ESSAYS IN INTERNATIONAL FINANCE

No. 197, June 1995

CURRENCY PROLIFERATION: THE MONETARY LEGACY OF THE SOVIET UNION

PATRICK CONWAY

INTERNATIONAL FINANCE SECTION

DEPARTMENT OF ECONOMICS
PRINCETON UNIVERSITY
PRINCETON, NEW JERSEY

INTERNATIONAL FINANCE SECTION
EDITORIAL STAFF

Peter B. Kenen, *Director*
Margaret B. Riccardi, *Editor*
Lillian Spais, *Editorial Aide*
Lalitha H. Chandra, *Subscriptions and Orders*

Library of Congress Cataloging-in-Publication Data

Conway, Patrick J.
 Currency proliferation: the monetary legacy of the Soviet Union / Patrick Conway.
 p. cm. — (Essays in international finance, ISSN 0071-142X ; no. 197)
 Includes bibliographical references.
 ISBN 0-88165-104-4 (pbk.) : $8.00
 1. Currency question—Former Soviet republics. 2. Monetary policy—Former Soviet republics. 3. Finance—Former Soviet republics. I. Title. II. Series.
HG136.P7 no. 197
[HG1075]
332′.042 s—dc20
[332.4′947]   95-18713
                                                                                                      CIP

Printed in the United States of America by Princeton University Printing Services at Princeton, New Jersey

International Standard Serial Number: 0071-142X
International Standard Book Number: 0-88165-104-4
Library of Congress Catalog Card Number: 95-18713

CONTENTS

FIGURES

TABLES

CURRENCY PROLIFERATION: THE MONETARY LEGACY OF THE SOVIET UNION

1 Introduction

The fifteen newly independent republics of the former Soviet Union began 1992 with a functioning ruble area inherited from the Soviet Union. Indeed, early that year, the ruble was atop the currency hit parade; no other currency served as sole legal tender across so many national borders.[1] The costs of maintaining the common currency turned out to be large, however, and despite the initial strong support for continuing the currency union, economies were flung from the ruble area as if by centrifugal force. By the beginning of 1994, only Russia and Tajikistan continued use of the ruble. All others had introduced new currencies, although Belarus had begun negotiations to return to the ruble.

This essay examines the centrifugal forces at work in the ruble area. Theory and past experience suggest that countries will choose to leave a currency area for three reasons: (1) nationalism, (2) a desire to insulate against monetary shocks originating in the economies of other members, and (3) a desire to increase national control over the collection of seigniorage from money creation. The non-Baltic nations among the former Soviet republics were predominately motivated by the desire for seigniorage. The Baltic nations were apparently driven by nationalism and a desire to insulate their economies from the monetary shocks caused by the excessive public-finance requirements of the non-Baltic members.

I thank Stanley Black and Richard Froyen for advice on improving this essay. I am grateful as well to Wafik Grais, Daniela Gressani, Françoise LeGall, and Chandrashekar Pant, at the World Bank, and to my in-country collaborators Bakhyt Abdildina, Alexander Bazarov, Irina Bazarova, Lali Kikalishvili, and Alla Suvorova for their excellent assistance in collecting data. Research for the essay was supported in part by a grant from the World Bank. The views expressed here, however, are the author's and not necessarily those of the World Bank or its staff.

[1] The CFA Franc is used as currency in thirteen countries, although there are technically two sets of banknotes, one issued for use in the seven West African countries and another issued for the six Central African countries.

1

The requirements of independence and the desire for gradual adjustment to the market economy combined to cause large and varying fiscal deficits in the non-Baltic members of the ruble area. Government control over the formal financial sector led to negative real interest rates on bank deposits and a consequent reduction of private saving in the banking system. Opportunities for international borrowing were also severely limited. The chief source of finance remaining to the governments was, therefore, seigniorage from the issue of money, and the non-Baltic members relied on this source. Whether the Central Bank of Russia (CBR), as issuer of rubles, could have accommodated these demands for seigniorage indefinitely remains an open question. In point of fact, it chose not to, and its limitations on currency issuance led to the introduction of "ruble supplements" in many member countries. The CBR's unwillingness to accept this credit creation by the non-Baltic central banks was evidenced by its imposition of limits on the convertibility of "non-cash" rubles in the correspondent accounts of those banks with the CBR. Its subsequent demands for more restrictive monetary policies in ruble-area countries led to the final decisions of the non-Baltic countries to break definitively with the ruble.

The Baltic nations, especially Estonia and Latvia, represent a different dynamic. From the time of independence, the governments of these countries had decided, for nationalistic reasons, that they would introduce independent currencies. Their determination was heightened as they recognized the inflationary effect of the search for seigniorage by the other members of the ruble area. The Baltic leaders realized that separate currencies would insulate their economies from these public-finance "shocks." Furthermore, because the Baltic governments had chosen a path of fiscal balance, they had no incentive to participate in the search for ruble seigniorage.

The ruble area quickly exhibited its signature difficulties of extreme inflation and disruptive commodity and financial arbitrage across borders. Although the non-Baltic members recognized these problems, they remained attached to the ruble for three reasons: (1) They were nostalgic for what they perceived as the Soviet economic success and confident that retaining the ruble would facilitate a return to the earlier form of economic integration; (2) they wished to continue exploiting the ruble system to collect seigniorage; and (3) they hoped to continue receiving "side payments" offered by the Russians in the form of intergovernmental credits and access to Russian energy resources at concessional prices. In the end, the anticipated gains dwindled, while the seigniorage available from participation in the ruble area proved insufficient to meet domestic fiscal needs.

Other difficulties also undermined the ruble area. The staggered timing of price and interest-rate liberalization across countries led to strong pressures for cross-border arbitrage. The governmental response was often a cessation of cross-border trade, despite its importance to sustained economic activity. There were also rigidities built into the financial system inherited from the Soviet Union, with banknotes and accounting credits circulating in two largely separate channels. These arrangements contributed to the economic distress, but their retention was itself the effect of the governments' search for seigniorage.

Section 2 examines the theoretical arguments bearing on the sustainability (and nonsustainability) of currency areas. Section 3 presents the main features of the ruble area before the breakup of the Soviet Union. Section 4 chronicles the competition for seigniorage after independence, and Section 5 describes the births of new currencies and the timing of these births with respect to the noncooperative forces at work within the ruble area.

2 Participation in a Currency Area

Participation in a currency area requires a specific monetary-policy decision of each member country. The country must agree to use the common currency as a unit of account and to accept banknotes of that currency as legal tender for official transactions. As a result, the banknotes have the attributes of money in each member country; they serve as unit of account, medium of exchange, and store of value. Residents of each member country are assured that their holdings of the currency will have purchasing power in the other members' markets.[2]

Institutions

Two institutions are usually associated with a currency area: a single monetary authority and a payments-clearing mechanism. The monetary authority will produce and distribute banknotes among the member

---

[2] Tavlas (1993) extended this notion to a monetary union that includes separate currencies under certain conditions regulating currency exchanges; these are: (1) the irrevocable fixing of parities, (2) the elimination of margins of fluctuations for exchange rates, (3) the total and irreversible convertibility of currencies (that is, the absence of exchange controls), and (4) the complete liberalization of both current and capital transactions. These four conditions are in principle implicit in the agreement to use a single currency.

3

countries. The banknotes become the liability of the authority, with government bonds or other claims as corresponding assets. The representatives designated by the authority to distribute the banknotes in each member country may be offices of the authority or may be the central banks of the member countries. In the latter case, the monetary authority supplies the banknotes in exchange for claims on the member countries' central banks. The United States and the former Soviet Union are examples of distribution through the offices of the monetary authority, with the U.S. states and Soviet republics in the role of "countries." The ruble area after the dissolution of the Soviet Union is an example of distribution through the members' central banks.

The payments-clearing mechanism provides a channel for settling non-banknote transactions within the currency area. The monetary authority is a natural location for this function because all the member central banks have accounting balances with it. Convertibility at par of all monetary instruments denominated in the common currency is a characteristic of a successful currency area. Within each country, there is convertibility between banknotes and accounting credits; across countries, there is convertibility of banknotes and also convertibility of accounting credits. As is demonstrated in the following sections, the disintegration of the ruble area is evident in the progressive breakdown of this convertibility.

Economic Gains

The economic gains from participation in a currency area accrue through increases in microeconomic efficiency, through sharing in the seigniorage of the combined area, or through payments made to individual countries for participation in the currency area. The distribution of such gains among the member countries may be either cooperative or noncooperative; the hallmark of the latter is the effort of individual members to manipulate the activity of the currency area to their own advantage.

Efficiency gains. The efficiency gains from participation are derived from the characteristics of trade and payments among those who will be members of the currency area. The literature has identified both benefits and costs of participation.[3] The major benefit is the assurance that gains from trade will not be dissipated by the costs of transacting

---

[3] Ishiyama (1975) provides a summary of the original discussions, and De Grauwe (1992), Goldstein et al. (1992), and Tavlas (1993) provide recent summaries of this literature. Eichengreen (1993) analyzes the efficiency gains of accession to the proposed European monetary union. Bayoumi (1994) provides a formal model of the microeconomic efficiency gains described in earlier research.

in foreign currencies or by an unanticipated change in the exchange rate. Canzoneri and Rogers (1990) define currency-conversion costs as the resource costs involved in conducting international trade in a number of currencies. The individual transactor will weigh the marginal gains from international trade against these marginal costs. With positive costs, international trade volume will less than fully exploit the potential gains from trade. Establishing a currency area removes the currency-conversion costs and allows the full exploitation of potential gains. The existence of multiple currencies also exposes international traders to the risk of exchange-rate variation. This variability will discourage trade by risk-averse traders and lead once again to smaller-than-potential welfare gains from international trade. Introduction of a single currency (or of a credibly fixed exchange rate) eliminates the risk of this variation and its discouraging impact on trade.

With respect to country-specific economic shocks, the use of a common currency is a two-edged sword. The currency serves as a channel for transmitting excess demand across member countries, because individuals unable to purchase a good in one country can use the common currency to purchase that good in another member country. Such transmission will be risk-reducing if economic shocks are industry specific and uncorrelated across countries. If one country has an inflationary situation, however, with excess demand for many goods, the common currency will reduce the initial country's realized inflation by transmitting the inflationary impulse to all member countries.

Shares of seigniorage. Seigniorage is the real value of resources transferred to a government through money growth.[4] It thus measures the increase in the government's real purchasing power that is attributable to money creation. Seigniorage rises with the rate of nominal money creation, but at a decreasing rate, owing to the accelerating rise in price inflation that the money creation engenders.[5]

In a currency area with a single monetary authority, the sharing of seigniorage among the participating countries will depend on the transactions protocol between the monetary authority and each country's

---

[4] I follow Blanchard and Fischer (1989, p. 179) in this definition, which includes the resource transfer from both increased real private holdings of money and the "inflation tax."

[5] There can in fact be a steady-state "Laffer curve" for seigniorage received through money creation, where a steady state is characterized by equality of actual and expected inflation (and monetary growth) rates. Evidence for the countries of the former Soviet Union does not indicate that this steady state has yet been attained; expected inflation appears to have lagged behind actual inflation during the first years of independence. Cukierman (1992) provides a useful summary of theoretical research in this field.

central bank. Casella (1992) analyzes the shares of seigniorage that will support a cooperative currency-area agreement in a two-country game. In her model, the gains from participating in the currency area accrue from the coordination of fiscal policy. However, a small country in a currency area will experience a welfare loss from participation if its share of seigniorage does not exceed its share of economic activity. By this reasoning, sustaining the currency area may well require that the monetary authority allow the small countries greater-than-proportional shares of seigniorage in order to ensure continued participation.[6]

Side payments. Corden (1972, p. 23) notes as particularly important the fiscal practice whereby "areas of monetary integration . . . use subsidies of various kinds to counter regional unemployment." Sala-i-Martin and Sachs (1992) provide evidence of this for the United States, where the tax and transfer activities of the U.S. fiscal system cushion one-third of the impact of region-specific shocks to disposable income. De Grauwe (1992) underlines the point for the state of Michigan with regard to the specific example of adjustment to the dual oil-price shocks of the 1970s, which disproportionately affected manufacturing in the U.S. "auto belt." As von Hagen (1992) notes, these (side) payments may be automatic—as in progressive tax-and-transfer fiscal systems—or they may be made in response to a specific economic shock.

Strategic manipulation. Each member of the currency area has a demand for seigniorage, but that demand is itself an endogenous weighing of the marginal welfare benefit of an increased fiscal deficit against the marginal welfare cost of increased inflation resulting from currency emission. In a cooperative setting, this weighing of costs and benefits will consider the currency area as a whole. Side payments among members or unbalanced seigniorage distributions by the monetary authority (as in Casella) can then ensure that each member is at least as well off as it would be in the absence of the currency area. The members' decision to refrain from issuing monetary instruments is the foundation for this cooperative equilibrium.

If each member of the currency area retains the ability to issue monetary instruments, there will be a strategic incentive to increase

---

[6] In Casella's model, this result is driven by the form of the utility function assumed. In noncooperative equilibrium, the smaller country places a larger proportion of its product in the public good. Because the public good is financed exclusively by seigniorage from money creation, the share of seigniorage in the smaller country must exceed its share in total product for the currency area in order to be welfare improving. Other welfare specifications may yield other conclusions.

seigniorage shares through monetary creation. This incentive is "free rider" in nature: money creation increases the real purchasing power of the domestic government, but the cost falls on holders of nominal assets throughout the currency area. Excess money creation occurs to set the marginal benefit of seigniorage equal to the marginal cost to the country's residents.[7] Ironically, seigniorage shares in equilibrium may be unaffected by this excess emission, for all members of the currency area will be similarly motivated.

Seigniorage, side payments, and strategic play: an illustration. The issues of seigniorage, side payments, and strategic play may be examined together within the following framework. There are I members of the currency area (indexed by i). Each member can be characterized in real terms by budgetary expenditures (g_i) and revenues (t_i) defining a budget deficit $(g_i - t_i)$. Each member can finance its deficit through intergovernmental extrabudgetary transfers (b_{gi}), increased debt to the public or the banking system $(\Delta D_i/P)$, and seigniorage (μ_i) from incremental monetary emission $(\mu_i = \Delta M_i/P)$. Equation (1) illustrates the relation of these in the government budget for member i. The financial instruments are defined in nominal terms and are deflated by the common price index (P) of the currency area:

$$(g_i - t_i) = b_{gi} + \Delta D_i/P + \mu_i \,. \tag{1}$$

Intergovernmental transfers may come from either inside or outside the currency area; I denote the total of transfers to members from outside the currency area as b, that is $\Sigma_{i=1}^{I} b_{gi} = b$. The total required seigniorage revenue from the currency area (μ) is then derived by summation of both sides of (1) and is presented as

$$\Sigma_{i=1}^{I}(g_i - t_i) - b - \Sigma_{i=1}^{I}\Delta D_i/P = \Sigma_{i=1}^{I}\mu_i = \mu \,. \tag{2}$$

Figure 1 illustrates the interaction between seigniorage and side payments in a two-country currency area with a single monetary authority; μ represents the total seigniorage amassed through currency emission.[8] The locus of possible allocations of that seigniorage between the two economies is shown by SS. The ray OR from the origin has a slope

---

[7] Buiter and Eaton (1983) give a good introduction to this phenomenon for a fixed-exchange-rate regime; Canzoneri and Henderson (1991) provide a more recent discussion.

[8] This real purchasing power is associated with either a specific value of P (for flexible prices) or rationing of goods (for fixed prices). As SS moves farther from the origin, it corresponds to a higher price level (and thus greater reduction of the value of nominal assets) within the currency area.

FIGURE 1
Seigniorage and Side Payments in a Currency Area

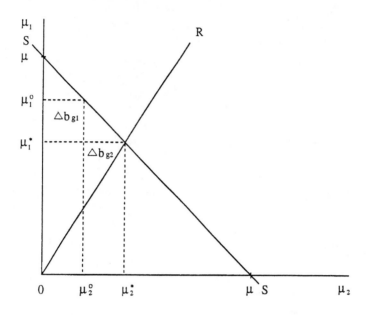

equal to the ratio of national products in the two economies, illustrating a "fair" allocation of seigniorage.[9] Suppose that the μ_i satisfying equation (1) for countries 1 and 2 are denoted by μ_i^o; in that case, there will be pressure within the currency area for a reallocation of seigniorage or for increased currency emission. This reallocation is achieved through a system of transfers (that is, $\Delta b_{g2} = -\Delta b_{g1}$) to ensure that fiscal needs are met without added pressure for currency creation. These transfers may be anticipated, as in the budgeting of the Soviet Union or in the below-market pricing of energy resources offered by Russia after independence. They may also be unanticipated, as occurred during the period of independence with correspondent-account overdrafts and zero-interest technical credits to clear those overdrafts (discussed below).

When each country has the ability to issue a monetary instrument, this illustration must be amended. A cooperative outcome can replicate that of the single monetary authority, but noncooperative outcomes are

---

[9] Alternative bases for allocation could be used, including shares based on relative bargaining power in the currency area. The Nash cooperative solution offers one such allocation. Friedman (1990, chap. 6) provides an overview of this and other bargaining outcomes.

8

also possible. In the noncooperative case, the marginal cost to member i of an increased fiscal deficit is reduced, because a portion of the inflationary effect is passed through trade to the other members of the currency area. Member i's preferred monetary emission (measured by the seigniorage attained) further depends upon the emission of the other members, because member j's emission imposes an inflationary cost on member i. Thus, as the demand for seigniorage by other members rises, demand by member i will fall.

The outcome of this strategic play is illustrated in Figure 2. Suppose that the central monetary authority continues to emit currency and to allocate seigniorage in the shares indicated by μ_i^*. The noncooperative emission schedules are represented by best-reply functions $m_1 m_1$ and $m_2 m_2$. The intercepts exceed μ_i^o by the amount of excess deficit spending by each member, and the functions are negatively sloped owing to the inflationary spillover across countries. A Nash noncooperative equilibrium is indicated by μ_i^n. Transfers are once again possible (along a line parallel to SS) to redistribute the seigniorage gains. This equilibrium is characterized by larger deficit spending, greater seigniorage, and greater shared inflation. As will be evident in the following sections, this characterization is consistent with behavior in the ruble area since independence.

FIGURE 2

STRATEGIC MANIPULATION IN A CURRENCY AREA

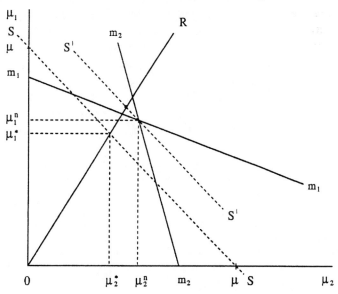

9

3 The Ruble Area in the Soviet Union

For the constituent republics of the Soviet Union, the ruble was the sole unit of account and medium of exchange. All financial instruments were denominated in rubles, and the ruble was convertible into foreign currencies at fixed exchange rates, although only through the activities of the Foreign Trade Bank and subject to substantial restrictions.[10] The traditional approach to financing Soviet fiscal deficits depended less on seigniorage than on borrowed funds from the private sector through the intermediation of the banking system; in the last years of the Soviet Union, however, the central government increased its reliance on seigniorage.

Economic Activity and Institutions in the Soviet Union

The Soviet economy was designed to magnify the gains from trade among the member republics. Production facilities were constructed on an extremely large scale, ensuring that a small number of plants could supply consumers and downstream producers in all the Soviet republics. Plants were more often sited to provide equitable allocations of production facilities across republics than to provide production at minimum cost. As a result, the production process for a single good involved many interrepublican transactions.

The limited number of producers may have only lightly burdened the central planners in Gosplan (the planning ministry), but the resulting flows of inputs and final goods among producers and consumers placed great responsibility on Gossnab (the supply ministry). As Figure 3 illustrates, the republics of the former Soviet Union were highly integrated with one another but not with other nations. Maintaining this interrepublican integration was especially critical to maintaining production levels because interrepublican trade included a large proportion of trade in production inputs. A disruption of trade among republics disrupted production in each of the republics.

Monetary authority and the financial system. The Gosbank was the monetary authority for the Soviet Union. Its policy of ruble-banknote emission was essentially passive. If the demand for currency to meet necessary wage and pension payments exceeded the stock of currency

---

[10] There was also during this period a unit of account called the "transferable ruble," which was used for clearing balances of payments among CMEA countries at the International Bank of Economic Cooperation in Moscow. The transferable ruble was neither strictly transferable nor strictly a ruble but was used to ensure the bilateral clearing of trade flows at prices determined by an average of past world market prices. It will not be considered further in this essay; see Kenen (1991) for additional detail.

FIGURE 3

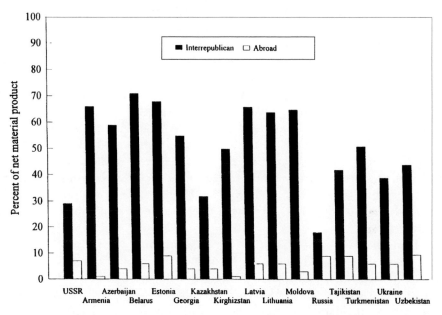

SOURCE: Hogan, "Economic Reforms in the Former Soviet Union," 1991.

available through the financial system, the Gosbank issued additional currency against the liabilities of the central government (Gregory and Stuart, 1990). Branches of the Gosbank handled financial duties in the individual republics; the republics did not have separate central banks.

Financial flows in the Soviet Union were designed to satisfy two goals: (1) The financial transactions of the production sector were to mirror and provide a check on the flows of real resources programmed by Gosplan for the production of goods and services, and (2) the financial sector was to mobilize household saving and make it available to the government for its investment activities. The financial-sector apparatus designed to achieve these goals had three features that were strikingly different from those in market economies. First, the Gosbank was the only bank for the entire economy; even after 1987, when it was broken into pieces, the activities of the pieces remained under the control of Gosbank leadership. Second, the use of currency and credit for making payments occurred in two largely separate channels. Third, government liabilities were the chief assets for the entire financial system.

The annual production plan not only specified the flows of real resources through the Soviet economy, it also specified the sizes and

11

means of payment for those resources. These payments were entered into accounts with the Gosbank (Ickes and Ryterman, 1994). Under the production plan, each enterprise was allocated working capital to complete its planned production. When the enterprise purchased inputs from another firm at the price specified in the plan, the supplier presented the Gosbank with the invoice, and an accounting transfer was made from the recipient's account to the supplier's account. When funds in the recipient's account were insufficient, the Gosbank provided credit to the recipient. Under the plan, the enterprise obtaining Gosbank credit would repay the amount with funds subsequently received in payment for its products. At the end of the plan period, the Gosbank "settled" the account by writing off any uncleared credit. No reserves were necessary in this system to settle imbalances in accounts. Enterprise profits were either taxed away by the government or deposited in time deposits at the Gosbank, where they received low nominal rates of interest.

Households received their wage, pension, and other transfer payments in currency. They could either purchase goods (when available) with this currency, save by depositing it with the Gosbank, or simply hold on to it. The saving deposits typically earned only 2 percent per annum in nominal return, but price inflation was insignificant until the last years of the Soviet Union. Households could make accounting payments for utilities and other government services through debits to their savings accounts.

The government received tax payments from households and enterprises and made pension and other transfer payments to households. It was also responsible for investment expenditures by enterprises. Budget balance was not required of the government; it financed any differences between expenditures and revenues through credits from the Gosbank.

Beginning in 1987, the Gosbank's operations were divided. The Gosbank retained the activities associated with central banks. The other financial operations were assigned to five state-owned specialized banks: the Saving Bank, Foreign Trade Bank, Industrial Bank, Agricultural Bank, and the Social Sector Bank. The formation of joint-stock banks was also permitted at this time. In 1989, the Gosbank formed a commercial banking department to regulate the nascent private financial sector and to set prudential standards for its operations. In 1991, the Industrial, Agricultural, and Social Sector Banks were reorganized as joint-stock corporations nominally independent of the government. The Saving Bank was made independent at the same time, but its reorganization was later reversed and the bank reabsorbed as a part of the Gosbank. Also in 1991, the Foreign Trade Bank was renamed the Bank for Foreign Economic Affairs and was absorbed into the Gosbank to manage the foreign-exchange transactions of the Soviet Union. Despite the organizational shifts, these specialized banks remained quite well integrated with the Gosbank for the purposes of currency flow and resource mobilization. The decentralization led to some difficulties, however, in the payments-clearing process. Many enterprises had not built up financial reserves to serve as working capital or to provide bridge financing between payments and receipts, and no single bank had the responsibility or the reserves to play this role. As a result, the buildup of arrears became a major aspect of the flow of funds.

The financial system of the Soviet Union served largely to finance expenditures by the Ministry of Finance, the obligations of which represented 72 percent of the central bank's assets in 1991 (Table 1). The bank's liabilities were dominated by refinance credit provided to the commercial and specialized banks. These credits tended to be "directed credits," that is, the commercial banks made the loans at the government's request and then refinanced them through the Gosbank.

In the Soviet banking system as a whole, 364.4 billion rubles had been

TABLE 1

THE GOSBANK BALANCE SHEET, JANUARY 1, 1991

(*billions of rubles*)

Assets		Liabilities and Net Worth	
Foreign exchange and precious metals	1.2	Banknotes and coins in circulation	136.1
Credit to commercial banks	119.5	Deposits of the government	20.2
Credit to the government	462.1	Correspondent balances and required reserves of commercial banks	39.1
Bonds	49.1	Deposits of enterprises and individuals	61.3
Other assets	6.5	Deposits of other (state) banks	368.8
		Paid-in capital and reserve funds	2.3
		Other liabilities	10.6
Total	638.4	Total	638.4

SOURCE: Goskomstat-USSR, *Narodnoe Khozaistvo SSSR v 1990 g*, p. 28 (1991). Aggregation by author.

13

issued in active credits at the beginning of 1991.[11] Of these, only 11.6 billion rubles (or 3 percent of the total) were extended to individuals; the rest were made available to enterprises and for government activities in short-term (75 percent) and long-term (22 percent) credits. At the same time, deposits of individuals with the Saving Bank totaled 381.4 billion rubles. This indicates an almost complete pass-through of saving to the government. A large part of the government's spending was investment related. In 1990, capital expenditures totaled 229.8 billion rubles, with an additional 39.1 billion rubles allocated to housing construction (data from Goskomstat-USSR, 1991).

Payments mechanism. This monobank system of accounts produced a dichotomy between banknote and accounting transactions in the flow of funds. Households received wages from enterprises and transfers from the government. They then used these to purchase goods and to save through deposits at the Gosbank. These flows took place in banknotes, or "cash rubles," using the Soviet terminology (McKinnon, 1991; Lipton and Sachs, 1992; Ickes and Ryterman, 1994). Financial flows among enterprises and between enterprises and the government occurred through accounting entries at the Gosbank and were thus in non-cash rubles. The cash and non-cash circuits were not completely self-contained or self-balancing, however, because the enterprise and banking sector received and made payments in both cash and non-cash rubles. The convertibility of cash and non-cash flows was ensured by the Gosbank, which exchanged banknotes and accounting rubles at par.

The coexistence of cash and non-cash transactions is not surprising; in most economies, both types of payments are honored. The striking feature in the Soviet system is the sharp dichotomy in their use. Household transactions were predominantly in banknotes; transactions between enterprises and the government were predominantly in accounting credits. In addition, banknotes played a more important role in the Soviet economy than in Western economies. In 1985, for example, currency in circulation as a share of gross national product (GNP) in the Soviet Union was 10 percent, or roughly double its share in the United States (Goskomstat-USSR, 1991; Council of Economic Advisors, 1993). The decentralization of the financial sector in 1987 and the following years introduced new institutions but no appreciable change in the flow of funds or of currency. Although the Gosbank's role was divided among nominally different financial institutions, effective control remained with the Gosbank leadership.

---

[11] Here and throughout, "billion" denotes a thousand million.

With the weakening of the Soviet government after the attempted coup against Gorbachev, the Central Bank of Russia (CBR) began to usurp the responsibilities of the Gosbank. During 1991, the Russian Supreme Soviet nationalized all banks on Russian soil. By the end of the year, Giorgi Matyukhin, head of the CBR, had established his own credit policy, ignoring that of the Gosbank. Russia assumed responsibility for emission of the ruble, as well as for the international payments-clearing mechanism, both of which had earlier been the responsibility of the Gosbank.

Weaknesses in the Ruble Area on the Eve of Independence

The last years of the Soviet Union saw increasing Soviet budget deficits. These were financed through foreign borrowing and through the seigniorage captured by the accelerating creation of money and credit. The process of money and credit creation generated excess demand for goods and services, but price controls transformed this demand into shortages of goods and services and increased the "forced" money and deposit holdings that represented the seigniorage received by the government.

Increasing budget deficits. Gorbachev's reforms of the production sector in 1987 relaxed the requirement that producers supply goods according to plan; producers were given greater leeway in determining production levels and markets for their goods. These were appropriate reforms, but they had a negative impact on output as producers scrambled to identify their own sources of inputs. Turnover taxes linked to production levels fell off, and the loss of this major share of tax revenues contributed to raising budget deficits.

In the 1990s, and especially in the aftermath of the attempted right-wing coup of 1991, the authority of Gorbachev and the government of the Soviet Union was challenged by the leaders of the constituent republics. Boris Yeltsin, of Russia, is the best known of these, but strident opposition to the continuation of Soviet power also came from Zviad Gamsakhurdia, of Georgia, Leonid Kravchuk, of Ukraine, and from the leaders of the Baltic states. These leaders pressed their claims by holding back from the center revenues collected within their republics.

The Soviet government had large fiscal responsibilities. Most notably, it was directly responsible for numerous vast industrial operations, including those in the defense and aerospace sectors. In the absence of adequate tax revenues, the government sought to sustain these operations by deficit spending through credit creation by the Gosbank (led by Viktor Geraschenko). The outcome of these activities was a large

15

buildup of inflationary pressure in the final years of the Soviet Union. In 1991, the aggregate fiscal deficit of the members of the Soviet Union reached 26 percent of gross domestic product (GDP).

Forced Financing: The Ruble Overhang. The Soviet Union of the late 1980s was characterized by price controls, public-sector borrowing needs in excess of private saving, and a disproportionate allocation of resources to national defense and the output of producer goods. Households and private enterprises, unable to purchase the quantities of goods and services desired, were "forced" to save. This saving took the form of both excess currency holdings and excess deposits in the financial system. The ratio of household liquid assets to household income rose from about 60 percent in the 1970s to about 95 percent in 1989.[12] This buildup became known among analysts as the "ruble overhang." Private-sector holdings of both currency and household deposits rose as a share of GNP from 1985 to 1990, with the currency share rising from 10 to 13 percent and household deposits rising from 29 to 37 percent.

The buildup of the ruble overhang was positively correlated with the mushrooming Soviet budget deficit and can be interpreted as the seigniorage used to finance that deficit. Table 2, drawn from McKinnon (1991), illustrates this correlation. Prior to 1986, the annual increase in household saving deposits was about equal to the government budget deficit. Subsequent to 1986, the budget deficit far exceeded the increase in saving deposits. The balance was made up through monetization. Despite currency emission during the 1987-89 period that raised the stock of currency by more than 13 percent a year, price controls ensured that retail inflation rates averaged under 3 percent a year (Dornbusch, 1992).

Commentators worried about the inflationary impact of price liberalization in this context. The solutions suggested can be organized into "demand-side" and "supply-side" policies. McKinnon (1991) focused on the demand side, suggesting that interest rates on deposits be raised to convert forced saving into desired saving and thus reduce currency hoarding. Proposals aimed at the supply side included the exchange of government assets and gold holdings for the excess currency and deposits.

---

[12] In economies with greater financial development, the government will finance budget deficits by issuing bonds. In the Soviet Union, the government used the banking system as the intermediary to channel resources to the government, and household deposits in the commercial banks (in addition to the hoarding of currency) became claims on the government.

TABLE 2

FINANCIAL STATISTICS FOR THE SOVIET ECONOMY

Year	Government Budget Deficit		Government Debt		Household Saving Deposits	
	Billions of Rubles	Percent of GNP	Billions of Rubles	Percent of GNP	Billions of rubles	Percent of Retail Sales
1980	12	1.9	76	12.2	156.5	57.9
1981	9	1.4	85	13.1	165.7	57.9
1982	15	2.2	100	14.4	174.3	58.9
1983	10	1.4	110	15.1	186.9	61.1
1984	9	1.2	119	15.7	202.1	63.9
1985	14	1.8	133	17.1	220.8	68.0
1986	46	5.8	179	22.4	242.8	73.1
1987	52	6.3	231	28.0	266.9	78.2
1988	81	9.3	312	35.7	296.7	81.0
1989	92	6.9	404	43.4	337.7	83.7

SOURCE: McKinnon, *The Order of Economic Liberalization*, table 11.1 (1991).

In January 1991, the Soviet government undertook a draconian supply-side policy by declaring that large-denomination bank notes would no longer be legal tender. Holders were allowed to exchange them for smaller bills up to a maximum governed by either their monthly salary or a fixed quantity, whichever was smaller. Household saving accounts were frozen, with individuals allowed to withdraw only 500 rubles a month. The net impact of this reform on inflation is by no means clear. Although the supply of money, broadly defined, was reduced, so was confidence in money as a store of value. Expenditure almost certainly rose as a consequence. Furthermore, inflation emerged overtly in 1991. A controlled increase in consumer prices during April led to price increases that averaged about 100 percent for the year, and the increase in wholesale price indices was roughly double that. Currency in circulation in the Soviet economy grew at the same pace.

4 The Ruble Area after Independence

With independence, the ruble area was adapted to the new political structure. Each republic established its own central bank based on the republican office of the former Gosbank. Each central bank then took responsibility for its national financial system. The CBR assumed the responsibilities of monetary authority for the currency area in addition to the activities of central bank for the Russian republic. The CBR was

17

the sole source of banknote emission for the ruble area and, through the correspondent accounts of the national central banks with the CBR, served as the area's payments clearinghouse.

The allocation of seigniorage within the currency area became an important source of conflict following independence. This conflict was due in part to independence itself. Not only did the republican governments inherit varying shares of the Soviet Union's expenditures, they lost the equilibrating budgetary transfers of the Soviet period. At the same time, the economic reforms that coincided with independence increased the need for seigniorage in the ruble area. New tax systems were not immediately as effective as the old had been, and liberalization of commodity and service prices ignited a tremendous burst of inflation that discouraged private saving in the banking system. Thus, the demands of member central banks for seigniorage were greatly increased.

The mechanism used for capturing seigniorage in the ruble area was quite similar to that found in textbooks, although some features must be amended to reflect the inherited Soviet structure of the ruble economies. In the textbook case, the government finances its fiscal deficit by placing debt instruments with the central bank. It receives in return cash or demand deposits drawn on the commercial banking system. The central bank receives the debt instrument as asset and issues cash or increases commercial-bank reserves as its liability. If households are willing to hold the increased money at current price levels, the resource transfer to the government is noninflationary. If households are unwilling to do so, the resulting excess demand for goods increases the price level until that stock of money is willingly held.

This is the mechanism that functioned in the ruble area, but the definition of government must be broadly extended. The ruble-area governments borrowed from the central banks to cover budget deficits, receiving non-cash credits at commercial banks. A major component of public excess demand, however, came from state enterprises not included in the state budget. The governments in the non-Baltic countries met the financing needs of these enterprises through "directed credits," that is, credits given to the enterprises by commercial banks and then refinanced by the central banks. The balance sheet of the central bank registered increased assets (the credit to the commercial bank) and increased liabilities (the reserves of the commercial bank) but did not absorb government debt. The commercial bank had the refinance credit of the central bank to offset its loan to the state enterprise, with the interest rate on the loan usually set just above that of the refinance credit to remove any interest-rate risk.

The definition of money must also be extended with regard to the ruble area. In textbook seigniorage, the government is not required to repay the debt. This freedom from future liability distinguishes seigniorage from debt issuance in public finance. In the ruble area, however, the liabilities of the government (and state enterprises) were nominally debt instruments, which require repayment. They were typically "directed," however, to have low or zero nominal interest rates and long maturities; in extreme inflation, this approximates the public-finance aspects of seigniorage. Inflation thus had a welfare cost, but a public-finance benefit, in the ruble area.

A successful currency area is characterized by the convertibility of monetary instruments within and among its members. Conversely, currency-area "fatigue" is manifest in an interruption of this convertibility. Inconvertibility in the ruble area was evident almost immediately after the dissolution of the Soviet Union. Within each republic, households and enterprises had great difficulty in converting existing bank deposits into banknotes; their inability to do so was termed the "cash shortage." Deficits on the correspondent accounts of the republic's central banks with the CBR appeared quickly and grew to immense size, triggering imposition by the CBR of limits on imbalances in these accounts and thus limiting as well the exchange at par of non-cash rubles between republics. Ruble supplements, locally circulated banknotes defined to trade at par with the ruble, were introduced in many ruble-area republics, but these were accepted at par only in the issuing country. By the end of 1992, the only assured exchange at par among, and within, member republics was in ruble banknotes.[13]

The speed with which convertibility within the ruble area broke down is attributable to the varying and often excessive emission of currency supplements and refinance credit by the member central banks. This pattern of excessive emission was the byproduct of large public-sector deficits combined with the unavailability of noninflationary financing for these deficits. This emission represented a demand for seigniorage in the member republics that greatly exceeded the supply provided by the CBR through the distribution of ruble banknotes.

The Rapid Rise in the Financing Requirement

The dissolution of the Soviet Union caused an intensification of the fiscal trends noted in the Gorbachev period. Government expenditure

[13] Even this convertibility was limited by the CBR's declaration in July 1993 that pre-1993 rubles would no longer be accepted as legal tender. This episode is discussed below.

rose and tax revenues fell in each of the former republics. In addition, budgetary transfers from the Soviet Union were no longer available. Finally, the continuing inflation coupled with nominal interest rates held at preinflation values greatly reduced the attractiveness of deposits held in the banking system.

The fiscal-policy choices made by the member republics placed them along a continuum of budget realization that extended from balance to extremely large deficits. As Figure 4 illustrates, the budget surplus as a share of GDP in seven former Soviet republics ranged from very negative to zero in mid-1993. The Baltic republics of Estonia and Lithuania implemented fiscal reforms that led to budgetary balance. The non-Baltic economies opted for large budget deficits, with those of Georgia and Ukraine taking on pathological dimensions. Because private saving was inadequate to finance these deficits, governments were driven to monetization to capture seigniorage and manipulation of correspondent balances to obtain long-term zero-interest loans. With liberalized prices, seigniorage came at the expense of extreme inflation.

FIGURE 4

FISCAL DEFICITS AND REAL INTEREST RATES IN SEVEN FORMER REPUBLICS

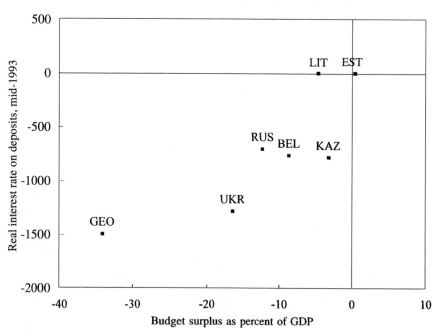

SOURCE: Author's data-collection network.

Reduced tax revenues. Five separate tendencies reinforced one another to cause a substantial fall in tax collection following independence. First, the downward trend in tax revenues relative to product value following production reform in 1987 accelerated as increasingly autonomous firms discovered ways to shelter profits from taxation. Second, the devolution of tax collection to the republican level caused a temporary loss in control over the process. Third, confusion consequent to the substitution of a value-added tax for the traditional turnover tax in many republics led to a loss of tax revenue. Fourth, the wholesale privatization of enterprises reduced the governments' knowledge of the taxable income of firms, allowing greater scope for evasion. The confluence of these tendencies is evident in Table 3 in the falling shares of GDP paid in tax revenues. Fifth, and of great importance, the collapse of output following independence reduced the taxable base for both production and consumption taxes.

TABLE 3

THE FISCAL STATUS OF THE FORMER SOVIET REPUBLICS
(percent of GDP)

Country	Revenues			Fiscal Deficit[a]		
	1991	1992	1993	1991	1992	1993
Belarus	47.6	42.8	44.8	3.7	6.4	8.4
Estonia	44.5	31.2	32.1	-4.4	-1.5	-0.4
Georgia	29.8	11.0	13.0[b]	3.5	28.0	34.0
Kazakhstan	25.0	24.6	22.7	7.9	7.3	3.0
Kirghizstan	35.2	15.8	16.4	4.8	16.5	10.1
Latvia	37.3	31.0	27.9	-6.3	-0.9	0.3
Lithuania	40.2	33.1	26.3	-2.3	-1.9	4.1
Moldova	25.3	20.0	11.4	0.0	26.0	6.1
Russia	—	40.8	—	16.5	14.2	—
Turkmenistan	38.0	45.0	22.0	-2.0	-14.0	7.0
Ukraine	40.3	42.5	24.5	13.6	27.8	16.3
Uzbekistan	49.1	33.5	34.7	3.6	13.0	15.8

SOURCES: For 1991 and 1992: International Monetary Fund, *International Financial Statistics*; for 1993, estimates from World Bank or IMF sources.

NOTE: General government definition, except for Moldova and Uzbekistan. Data are incomplete for Russia and unavailable for Armenia, Azerbaijan, and Tajikistan.

[a] Positive entries indicate fiscal deficits.

[b] Includes grants; revenues excluding grants were 3 percent of GDP.

The role of privatization and corporate autonomy in the fall of tax revenues is illustrated by Belarus and Kazakhstan, the two republics in which tax revenues did not fall significantly. Belarus experienced roughly constant shares of tax revenues in GDP from 1991 to 1993, in large part because it continued to support the state enterprise system; the first steps toward privatization of production in 1994 reportedly caused large drops in tax revenues. In Kazakhstan, which experienced only a minor downturn in the share of tax revenue in GNP in 1992-93, privatization of production facilities occurred quite slowly. President Nursultan Nazarbayev of Kazakhstan stated in March 1994 that it would be twenty-five to thirty years before the state sector's share in the economy would fall below 50 percent (Rutland and Isataev, 1995).

Increased public deficits. The independent republics were predisposed to continuing the budget deficits from the Gorbachev regime. Although expenditures were excessive in the final years of the Soviet Union, citizens had become accustomed to the level of benefits they received. With the dissolution of the Soviet Union, moreover, most Soviet state enterprises became the budgetary responsibility of the republic in which they operated; at the same time, transfers from the Soviet budget disappeared.

Table 3 indicates the magnitude of the fiscal deficits of various former republics. There is a clear tendency toward greater fiscal deficit in the non-Russian republics in 1992, with only Kazakhstan and Turkmenistan moving in the opposite direction. In 1993, there was substantial regression toward a mean. Estonia retained a surplus, while the republics with the largest deficits were able to reduce their fiscal imbalances. These deficits remained large, however, and required substantial domestic finance.

As noted above, the state budgets reflected only part of the total expenditure managed by the governments. The governments of these republics often implemented public-sector expenditure programs by instructing state-owned commercial banks (for example, the republican successors to the Industrial or Agricultural Bank) to provide "directed credits" to specific state enterprises. These credits were in turn refinanced by the central banks at strongly negative real interest rates and at maturities greater than six months. As a result, they represented seigniorage resource transfers nearly equal to their face value. The growth in domestic credit is shown in Table 4 for various former republics; in all the republics, growth in domestic credit was more rapid than growth in deposit creation.

Financial disintermediation. The real value of deposits in the commercial banking systems of the former Soviet republics dropped sharply

TABLE 4

CREDIT, CURRENCY, AND DEPOSIT CREATION IN SIX FORMER
REPUBLICS

| | Billions of Rubles | Percent Increase over End-1991 | | |
	End-1991	Mid-1992	End-1992	Mid-1993
Belarus				
Domestic credit[a]	48.6	240	850	4,676
Currency	4.7	230	713	3,963
Deposits	47.7	112	60	1,512
Georgia				
Domestic credit	27.4	73	824	1,608
Currency	6.1	53	397	1,923
Deposits	14.8	11	291	784
Kazakhstan				
Domestic credit	68.0	290	1,366	4,550
Currency	14.0	125	1,002	3,791
Deposits	69.9	28	663	1,952
Lithuania[b]				
Domestic credit	10.5	204	588	925
Currency	7.4	35	149	296
Deposits	19.7	86	411	518
Russia				
Domestic credit	895.0	152	826	2,062
Currency	167.0	168	1,011	3,158
Deposits	1,034.0	130	905	2,050
Ukraine				
Domestic credit	250.4	386	1,671	6,023
Currency	33.8	399	1,815	5,776
Deposits	229.4	166	789	3,431

SOURCE: International Monetary Fund, *International Financial Statistics: Supplement on Countries of the Former Soviet Union* (1993).

[a] Domestic credit refers to "net claims on government" plus "claims on rest of economy."

[b] Figures for mid-1993, evaluated at end of May.

after independence. Table 4 provides details of the rate of nominal deposit creation in selected republics. Growth rose in nominal terms, but it was greatly exceeded by the inflation rate. In real terms, then, there was disintermediation,[14] in that the real value of saving made

---

[14] Real disintermediation acts differently than inflation on the value of the stock of nominal financial instruments. The extreme inflation of 1992 removed the "ruble overhang"

available through deposits in the financial sector after independence was reduced relative to its preindependence level.

Inflation reduced the real interest rates on saving deposits and certificates of deposit to sharply negative values (the annual nominal deposit rates and monthly inflation rates shown in Table 5 for selected republics in mid-1993 are used to derive the real interest rates shown in Figure 4). Competition for funds could be expected to drive up these negative real interest rates, but there was little evidence of such competition. Because the major source of funds to the commercial banks was refinance credit from the central bank at low nominal interest rates, the commercial banks had little incentive to encourage private deposits. The lack of competition for deposits in Ukraine is illustrated by the large disparities in the nominal annual interest rates quoted for deposits by various banks in mid-1993 (*Ukrainian Business News*, June 25, 1993):

Kiev:	Ukraina Bank	120 percent
	Prominvest Bank	74 percent
Lvov:	Dniester Bank	200 percent
	Elektronbank	220 percent
Odessa:	Feb Bank	180 percent

Conway (1994b) provides a more detailed analysis of these disparities and of the effect of government policies on the incentives to deposit-taking by formal financial intermediaries in the unsettled financial environment of the former Soviet Union.

Restrictions on the convertibility of deposits into cash also encouraged real disintermediation. Withdrawal rights were limited in the Soviet Union during the indexation of April 1991 and in ruble-area members at various times after independence. The rationing scheme in Georgia is illustrative. A National Bank of Georgia (NBG) regulation on June 1, 1992, stated three rules for withdrawals. Cooperatives and nongovernmental enterprises were allowed to withdraw in cash only that amount deposited as cash after April 1, 1992. Citizens with accounts at the Saving Bank could withdraw only that amount corresponding to current

---

in that it greatly reduced the real purchasing power of currency and deposits held by households. Real disintermediation, however, refers to the reduced flow of real resources into the banking system from period to period. The two are obviously related; if inflation erodes the purchasing power of existing banking deposits, households will be less likely to consign new real saving to the care of the banking system.

24

TABLE 5

NOMINAL ANNUAL INTEREST RATES ON SAVING AND LENDING IN SIX FORMER
REPUBLICS IN 1993, DOMESTIC CURRENCY ACCOUNTS

	Belarus June 30	Georgia June 30	Kazakhstan June 30	Lithuania June 10[a]	Russia June 23	Ukraine June 30
Saving Bank Deposits						
Sight	20	5	15	22	—	30
Less than 1 year	—	—	—	65–79	140	220
1 to 3 years	40	15	30	65–80	—	220
Loans						
Refinance credits[b]	100	20	25	—	—	240
1 year commercial	200	65	200	150	200	280
Auction rate	200	—	163–177	160–175	165–171	—
Monthly inflation rate[c]	30	40	35	13 & 1	19	21

SOURCES: Saving Bank successor agencies in each republic; reports from correspondents; news reports.

NOTE: Commercial banks were the Promstroi Bank for Belarus and Georgia, the Kazkommertsbank for Kazakhstan, the Aurabank for Lithuania, and the Elektronbank of Lvov for Ukraine. The figures for Russia are those reported as regional averages for Saratov in *Financial Isvestiya*, June 19–25, 1993.

[a] In Lithuania, deposit rates vary by number of months of obligation and size of deposit. Lending rates differ by source: 60 percent for central-bank credits, 60 to 90 percent for household credits, and 160 percent for enterprise credits.

[b] A typical refinance agreement is quoted. The interest rate on these is negotiated on a case-by-case basis in some countries.

[c] Monthly inflation rates are taken for the last available month before the observed interest rate, that is, May for Georgia, Kazakhstan, Lithuania, Russia, and Ukraine, and June for Belarus. For Lithuania, I also report the much lower rate for August, expectations of which may have been incorporated into the deposit and loan rates.

wage and pension payments deposited directly at the bank by their employers. State enterprises were exempt from limits on cash withdrawals. Saving and time deposits were thus much less liquid than currency.

The restrictions on convertibility were imposed in response to cash shortages, which were themselves a product of financial disintermediation. The policy response thus only aggravated the shortages. In addition, in a number of republics, cash shortages led enterprises to deposit wages in part directly into the banks—from which withdrawal was limited; these "forced deposits" account for a substantial part of the deposit growth observed for the period. Firms faced an additional disincentive to deposit in the banking system, because the government used bank records for the collection of value-added and other taxes.

Thus, despite the urgent need for additional private saving to finance government deficits, low nominal interest rates and controls on withdrawals made the banks unattractive depositories for saving.

Ruble Emission by the Central Bank of Russia

The Gosbank (and later the CBR) followed a policy in 1991 of validating price increases through cash emission, with the result that the consumer price indices (CPIs) and the stock of cash in circulation roughly doubled during the year. Massive cash shortages were nevertheless reported from all the republics soon after independence in January 1992. Price liberalization in the presence of the ruble overhang led to an increase of nearly 500 percent in the CPI during the first quarter of 1992, but the stock of cash in circulation throughout the ruble area rose by only 36 percent. For the rest of 1992, the rate of cash emission exceeded the inflation rate, but not by enough to validate completely the price inflation. For the year as a whole, consumption prices rose 2,300 percent, and ruble banknotes in circulation increased by 700 percent. During the first seven months of 1993, the stock of rubles in circulation in Russia further increased by an additional 125 percent, the stock of rubles transferred to member central banks rose by 56 percent, and the CPI in Russia increased by nearly 300 percent. Through the entire period, then, the stock of rubles in circulation failed to keep pace with the rate of inflation and to avert cash shortages throughout the ruble area.[15]

Despite the increased areawide demand for ruble banknotes, the CBR altered the historical pattern of ruble allocation to favor Russian destinations. In 1990-91, Russia received 66 percent of the rubles emitted by the Gosbank (*Kommersant*, May 18, 1992). By the first quarter of 1992, Russia was receiving 80 percent of the rubles, and in the first half of 1993, it received an even greater percentage.

The per capita distribution of currency among the other republics in the first seven months of 1993 was also quite uneven (see Table 6). Favorable treatment was accorded to Kazakhstan and Turkmenistan, whereas Azerbaijan and Georgia were treated poorly. (Estonia, Latvia, and Lithuania had removed rubles from circulation by this time.) Russia received 81 percent of total emission, although its population percentage

---

[15] The data reported in this paragraph are drawn from *Financial Isvestiya* (August 11, 1993), from statistics of the Macroeconomics and Finance Unit of Russia, and from the *Bulletin of Banking Statistics* of the CBR. In earlier work, I discussed the possibility of sustained inflation at a rate below that of money growth (Conway, 1994c).

TABLE 6

DISTRIBUTIONS OF CASH RUBLES AND RUSSIAN TECHNICAL
CREDITS IN THE FIRST HALF OF 1993
(*percent of total for period*)

Republic	Population (1989)	Bank Credit (1989)	Cash Rubles[a]	Technical Credits[b]
Armenia	1.1	1.2	0.5	1.1
Azerbaijan	2.5	2.0	0.1	0.7
Belarus	3.6	3.0	1.7	9.0
Estonia	0.5	0.4	0.0	0.0
Georgia	1.9	2.4	0.0	0.0
Kazakhstan	5.8	7.7	8.5	33.6
Kirghizstan	1.5	1.1	0.7	3.9
Latvia	0.9	0.9	0.0	0.0
Lithuania	1.3	1.3	0.0	0.0
Moldova	1.5	1.1	0.4	2.1
Russia	51.3	59.3	81.2	—
Tajikistan	1.8	0.8	0.6	5.1
Turkmenistan	1.2	0.9	2.0	3.4
Ukraine	18.0	13.4	0.0	21.1
Uzbekistan	6.9	4.5	4.3	20.1
Total	100.0	100.0	100.0	100.0

SOURCES: Russian Ministry of Finance; Center for Economic Reform; Goskomstat-USSR, *Narodnoe Khozaistvo SSSR v 1990 g*, p. 30
(1991).

NOTE: Numbers are rounded and may not add up to totals.

[a] Measured from January 1 to July 28, 1993, for all except Russia,
for which they are measured from January 1 to July 31, 1993.

[b] Issued from January 1 to June 30, 1993.

was just over 50 percent.[16] The allocation of bank credit within the
Soviet Union in 1989 is reported in column three of Table 6 to provide
a comparison based on financial activity. This allocation differed
somewhat from the population percentages, but not nearly to the extent
that currency allocations did in 1992 and 1993.

The Competition for Seigniorage and the Inconvertibility of Rubles

The Baltic and non-Baltic republics responded very differently to the
incipient financing shortfalls at the time of independence. The Baltic

[16] A number of countries, including Belarus, Georgia, and Ukraine, had issued ruble
supplements during this period. This altered the observed distribution of rubles but was
itself caused in part by that skewed distribution.

27

republics insisted on reductions in government expenditures to balance the shortfalls in resources. The non-Baltic republics financed the shortfalls, to various degrees, by credits refinanced through their central banks. This practice provided the governments and their state enterprises with purchasing power; once used, however, it inflated the ruble-denominated balances of depositors in the banking system. The corresponding seigniorage was extracted in one of two ways. If depositors' balances were convertible into cash or into purchasing power in other member countries, the seigniorage was extracted through the "inflation tax." If the balances were inconvertible (for reasons discussed below), the seigniorage was extracted from the depositors who had to hold the non-cash balances. To ensure convertibility into cash, many member countries introduced ruble supplements to circulate alongside ruble banknotes.

Credit creation and ruble supplements introduced strategic competition in monetary instruments (as described in Section 2). Each member could capture seigniorage by creating credits that its citizens or the citizens of other member countries would accept at par. With liberalized prices, however, the consequence of this policy was continuing inflation, cash shortages, and the inconvertibility of non-cash credits among member countries. Ukraine, for example, had a government budget deficit equal to 28 percent of GNP in 1992 and financed it through the issuance of 1.3 trillion rubles in credit by the National Bank of Ukraine (NBU).[17] Other members participated in this practice as well.

Budget deficits were also financed through the accumulation of arrears by governments in scheduled payments to their own citizens. This forced saving placed an onerous burden on the "recipients" in periods of high inflation.

Cash shortages. Cash shortages were reported throughout the ruble area, and the features were strikingly similar across countries. Producers and governments had limited access to cash through their financial accounts and so could not pay wages, pensions, and intermediate-input suppliers in cash. Wage earners and pensioners thus received insufficient cash to purchase products; producers consequently shut down or ran arrears with suppliers; and suppliers, in turn, either shut down or ran arrears with their workers and suppliers. The problem was exacerbated by the rapid rise in retail prices throughout the ruble zone. A premium for cash rubles relative to non-cash credits arose in the financial intermediaries.[18]

---

[17] The budget deficit figure is taken from Table 3; *The Economist* (March 13, 1993, p. 56) reported a budget deficit equal to 44 percent of GDP.

[18] Evidence of ruble shortages predates the dissolution of the Soviet Union. Even

Those receiving bank credits in payment for goods or services pressed the banking system to convert the non-cash deposits into cash. Because redepositing of cash was insufficient, however, the banking system was forced to ration conversions. This rationing produced cash shortages that transferred the cost of seigniorage to enterprises and households holding bank credits. Although the value of these credits eroded rapidly with inflation, they could not be converted into more liquid assets.

Table 7 provides a chronology of cash shortages in seven of the former Soviet republics. These republics can be separated into three groups. In Georgia and Ukraine, cash shortages were endemic throughout 1992 and 1993. In Belarus, Kazakhstan, Lithuania, and Russia, the shortages became acute in the spring of 1992 but subsided in the fall, although Belarus, Kazakhstan, and Lithuania suffered an additional episode of shortages in May and June of 1993. In Estonia, there were ruble shortages prior to the introduction of a new currency in June 1992, but there have been no cash shortages since then.

When non-cash credits are not freely convertible into cash, a rule is required to ration the demand for conversion. In some of the republics, this was at the discretion of the banking system. In others, it was controlled by government regulations. Georgia's three-tiered system for withdrawals exemplifies one set of regulations. Kazakhstan introduced similar restrictions in February 1992 and renewed them in June 1993. One feature of Georgia's restrictions was the automatic deposit of 30 percent of private wage earnings into banking-system deposits, which in most cases were then inconvertible into cash. The innovation in Kazakhstan's restrictions was the declaration that all shops must introduce cash registers for cash trade; the evident hope was that the machines would allow for a more accurate tracking of cash flows (Kazakhstan, Cabinet of Ministers, June 8, 1993).

Inconvertibility led to a premium in the informal trade of cash for accounting credits. In Belarus, for example, "obnalichka" dealers converted bank credits to cash for a 30 percent fee (*Minsk Economic News*, July 1993). These dealers exploited personal contacts they had made with the management and staff of banks to circumvent the regulations or "jump the queue" of those legally entitled to the scarce cash. Alternatively, this exchange could occur in a triangular fashion

---

during the period of stable prices before 1991, there was an excess demand for cash relative to non-cash rubles. This was due to the value of cash in untraceable transactions and led to a premium on cash rubles of roughly 10 percent.

TABLE 7

THE CHRONOLOGY OF CURRENCY SHORTAGES IN SEVEN
FORMER REPUBLICS

Republic	Period	Sources and Effects of Shortages
Belarus	May 1992	Wage arrears of 4 billion rubles
	March 1993	Ruble shortage; currency flight
	May-July 1993	Wage arrears
Estonia	March 1992	Ruble shortage requires sale of hard-currency reserves
Georgia	May-December 1992	Severe wage and pension arrears
	January-April 1993	Wage and pension arrears; 60 to 80 percent of consumers attempting to purchase on account
Kazakhstan	February-March 1992	Cabinet of Ministers issues edicts 148 and 300 limiting cash withdrawals from bank accounts
	May-August 1992	Wage and benefit arrears increasing from 6 to 15.4 billion rubles
	May-September 1993	Ruble shortfall; many firms on brink of strikes in July owing to wage arrears; "new" Russian rubles not yet accepted as legal tender, despite entry into circulation through trade with Russia.
Lithuania	February 1992	Monthly salaries of government officials not paid, including salary of prime minister
	May 1992	Wage and pension arrears of 3 billion rubles
	May-June 1993	Talonas shortfall, in part owing to withdrawal of counterfeit banknotes in circulation
Russia	December 1991- January 1992	CBR short 12 billion rubles; Russian Supreme Soviet restricts cash use and withdrawals
	May 1992	Wage and benefit arrears of 2 trillion rubles
	June 1992	Kuzbass workers and FNPR trade union threaten strike over nonpayment of wages
Ukraine	January 1992	Ruble shortage equal to 25 percent of wage payments leads to introduction of coupon
	June-August 1993	Widespread currency shortages lead to restrictions on currency withdrawal and use

SOURCES: Individual months are from news accounts; ranges are from data collected by in-country collaborators.

through the foreign-exchange markets. Table 8 illustrates this point with premia drawn from the foreign-exchange markets in Belarus, Georgia, and Kazakhstan. These were the premia implied by enterprise transactions converting both cash and non-cash credits into foreign exchange. Similar premia existed for the direct conversion of accounting credits to cash.

TABLE 8

THE PREMIA FOR CASH OVER NON-CASH CREDITS
IN BELARUS, GEORGIA, AND KAZAKHSTAN
(percent)

Republic	Date	Premium
Belarus	June 12, 1993	80
	August 15, 1993	15
	November 3, 1993	510
Georgia	April 1, 1993	669
	June 18, 1993	12
	October 4, 1993	154
Kazakhstan	June 16, 1992	35
	December 15, 1992	15
	May 20, 1993	34
	August 24, 1993	37

SOURCES: News reports and daily in-country
data collection.
NOTE: Premia are calculated from exchange
rates of each currency with U.S. dollar.

Correspondent imbalances. Unfinanced public-sector deficits cause an excess demand for goods and services. In an open economy, this excess demand can be satisfied in a noninflationary way if indebtedness to foreign creditors is possible.[19] In the ruble area, this indebtedness could be either to Western sources or to fellow members. The Baltic states were relatively successful in obtaining Western financing, although they employed it mainly to build up foreign-exchange reserves. The non-Baltic states, however, were limited to the funds made available by the World Bank, European Union (EU), and International Monetary Fund (IMF), and the amounts allocated by these organizations were small relative to the sizes of the states' fiscal deficits.

The competition for seigniorage crossed national borders when recipients of directed credits used them to purchase goods and services in other countries of the ruble area. Consider a hypothetical state enterprise in Georgia to which bank credit is extended (refinanced by the NBG) to purchase natural gas from Turkmenistan. The payment is made through the payments-clearing mechanism at the CBR, with the correspondent accounts of Georgia and Turkmenistan debited and credited, respectively. For Georgia, a sustained public-sector deficit

[19] Although noninflationary, such indebtedness requires debt-service payments in subsequent years, thus reducing the government's capacity to spend in the future.

financed through credit creation in excess of that in the rest of the currency area will lead to an imbalance in purchases of goods from other ruble-area countries and a negative balance, or overdraft, on its correspondent account. Domestic inflation will be limited, because excess demand for goods and services will spill over into other member economies. Seigniorage will be increased in Georgia through the increase in the real value of holdings of its liabilities—in this case, correspondent overdrafts of the other member countries.

The amount of ruble-denominated external financing was significant, especially in financing flows of goods from Russia to the other member countries. The Russian Ministry of Finance estimated that the equivalent of $17 billion, or over 10 percent of Russian GDP, was transferred through export subsidies or explicit lending agreements in 1992 (*ITAR-TASS*, July 13, 1993). In the first six months of 1992, the fourteen non-Russian republics in the ruble zone used these credits for a substantial share of their financing needs. These overdrafts were initially penalty free and at zero nominal interest rates and thus represented an attractive source of finance in a high-inflation environment.

Full convertibility of ruble credits across member countries required the unconditional acceptance of these correspondent imbalances. The imbalances were, however, very large. In the first half of 1992, the non-Russian republics accumulated correspondent-account (and thus trade-account) deficits totaling 320 billion rubles, equivalent to 67 percent of their exports to Russia (*The Economist*, September 19, 1992, p. 96). These deficits were automatically financed with "technical credits" provided by the Russian government to the CBR to balance the correspondent accounts with those countries.

The CBR recognized the unsustainability of this situation, given the financing needs of the member republics. On July 1, 1992, the CBR insisted that the NBU maintain balance in its correspondent account. The Russian government softened the blow of this decision by providing a (seemingly) large 10 billion ruble technical credit to build up Ukraine's correspondent balance. Unfortunately, because Ukraine's exports to Russia were so small relative to its imports, the credit was spent within one week. The limit imposed by the CBR, however, was binding, leading to the inconvertibility of ruble credits from Ukraine into Russian credits. Later in 1992, the CBR extended the same requirement to the correspondent imbalances of all the members of the ruble area.

Once overdrafts were limited, non-cash credits became inconvertible across countries, and secondary markets developed in these credits. At the end of August 1992, non-cash credits from non-Baltic economies traded at a discount to credits in Latvian rubles. In some cases, the discounts were small: the price for 100 non-cash Russian-ruble credits was 95 Latvian-ruble credits. In other cases, they were large: the price for 100 Kazakhstan- or Ukrainian-ruble credits was 30 Latvian-ruble credits. The non-cash credits of the non-Baltic countries all traded at a discount to those of Russia. By the end of January 1993, the discounts had widened for all ruble-area countries relative to Latvia and remained the same for the non-Baltic members relative to Russia (*The Economist*, September 19, 1992; *Financial Isvestiya*, January 20, 1993).

Ruble supplements. In a number of member countries, the cash shortages of early 1992 led to the introduction of ruble supplements or national currencies that were meant to trade at par with the ruble and to be freely exchangeable for rubles in transactions. Ukraine introduced the karbovanets in January 1992; Belarus, Latvia, and Lithuania introduced the zaichik, Latvian ruble, and talonas in May 1992; and Azerbaijan introduced the manat in August 1992. Georgia maintained exclusive use of the ruble until April 1993, when it introduced the menati.

The motivation for introducing supplements varied by region. In the Baltic states, the introduction of ruble supplements was the first step in a planned delinking from the ruble area. Latvia and Lithuania proceeded gradually by introducing supplements that eventually became sole legal tender and were subsequently replaced by permanent national currencies. Estonia broke with the currency area in one step in June 1992 by introducing a national currency (the kroon) linked to the German mark. In other member states, the ruble supplement was initially simply a response to cash shortages but over time took on the features of a national currency. Ukraine delinked the karbovanets from the ruble in November 1992, although it had not, by the end of 1994, introduced a permanent currency. Azerbaijan made the manat its sole legal tender in June 1993. Kirghizstan broke from the currency area in May 1993 by introducing the som as sole legal tender. Georgia made the menati sole legal tender in August 1993, and Belarus followed suit with the zaichik in late 1993. In these latter cases, the introduction of ruble supplements made possible the independent exploitation of seigniorage through the "textbook mechanism."

The Ambivalent Russian Response to Ruble-Area Fatigue

As cash shortages, correspondent overdrafts, ruble supplements, and other manifestations of monetary inconvertibility occurred within the ruble area, the CBR's response was ambivalent. The CBR held two potentially conflicting roles in the currency area. As monetary authority, it was responsible for an appropriate allocation of seigniorage among the member nations in the ruble area. As central bank for Russia, it was charged with ensuring both adequate seigniorage for the Russian fiscal deficit and adequate liquidity for Russian monetary transactions.

During the first years of independence, the Russian government was unable to finance its borrowing requirements through domestic saving or foreign borrowing. As a result, it relied upon credit creation ratified by CBR monetary expansion. The CBR's chairman, Viktor Geraschenko, became one of the most powerful and controversial men in Russia. Until September 1993, the CBR was accountable by law to both the Russian parliament and the presidency; after that time, it was to be accountable to the presidency alone. In fact, throughout this period, the CBR appeared to be operating quite autonomously.[20]

The CBR's actions indicate a desire to maintain the ruble area, but on terms favorable to Russia. Its allocations of ruble emission tended to favor Russian interests. Its insistence on monetary reform in member countries offered the Russian financial sector as a model and upheld CBR dominance of monetary policy. The CBR and the Russian government initially supported the ruble area through the acceptance of correspondent overdrafts unfavorable to Russia and through the extension of "technical credits" at zero nominal interest rates to clear those overdrafts. As the imbalances became larger and more costly, however, Russia placed limits on overdrafts. It later insisted on denominating the credits in U.S. dollars and charging positive real interest rates. These actions removed the subsidy to continued participation in the currency area and increased the incentive for members to leave.

The change in the CBR's approach to the ruble area mirrored that of the international financial organizations. The IMF and the World Bank initially supported preserving the ruble area but shifted in mid-1993 to encouraging the introduction of national currencies. Once international support shifted, and the costs to Russia of maintaining the ruble area became clear, the Russian reformist factions, who had favored dissolution of the ruble area since 1991, took the lead.

The increasing cost of settling correspondent overdrafts. Until May 1992, commercial banks had undertaken much of the clearing of

---

[20] Geraschenko was charged at various times in 1993 with corruption, disobedience, and sedition. In July 1993, the CBR was criticized in a Russian parliamentary investigation for having lax controls that permitted large-scale embezzlement. At about the same time, Anders Åslund (Radio Liberty Daily Report No. 144, July 30, 1993) cited "circumstantial evidence" of anomalous cash distributions of 588 billion rubles to former Soviet republics from April to June 1993.

balances through subsidiaries in other member countries or through correspondent relations between commercial banks. The large imbalances in the issuance of non-cash credits among member governments caused Russian financial institutions to hold substantial credit positions against the other currency-area members. The actual size of the capital-account imbalance, however, was concealed by the dispersion of these credit positions across many financial institutions. In May 1992, the CBR insisted that all transactions among member countries be passed through the centralized correspondent accounts at the CBR.

In July, the CBR imposed ceilings on the size of overdrafts allowed in these correspondent accounts. When negative balances in excess of the ceilings occurred, the accounting transfers for those excess transactions were not undertaken immediately but were set aside until sufficient positive flows brought the overdrafts under the ceiling. Once introduced, these ceilings were quickly and continually binding, despite substantial credit creation by the CBR. In the last half of 1992, the Russian government tripled its credits to the other republics in nominal terms, raising them to a year-end total of just over 1 trillion rubles. This trend continued into the first half of 1993. The credits offset the inability of the other republics to pay and papered over the problem of arrears from purchasers in those countries. Belarus is a case in point. In 1991, Belarus had a 5 billion ruble trade surplus with the states of the ruble area. In 1992, however, it had a 37 billion ruble trade deficit; the trade deficit with Russia totaled 63 billion rubles. The deficit with Russia was financed by a reduction in the correspondent balance of the National Bank of Belarus (NBB) and a technical credit from the Russian government for that part of the deficit that was in excess of the ceiling. In 1992 and during the first half of 1993, Russia provided a total of 230 billion rubles (80 billion in 1992, 150 billion in 1993) in technical credits to allow Belarus to run trade deficits with Russia.[21] These credits bore no interest rate and were not to mature until 1996.

In mid-1993, Russia decreed that any overdraft had to be financed by intergovernmental (state) credits at a positive interest rate and with a shorter maturity; in addition, Russia could choose not to offer these credits at all. Table 9 indicates the allocations and terms of these state credits in mid-1993. In May 1993, for example, when Belarus could not

[21] The figures on the trade deficit are drawn from NBB and State Committee on Statistics sources. The figures on technical credits were obtained in personal interviews. The discrepancy between 63 and 80 billion rubles may be due to rounding or to additional technical credits issued to cover NBB liabilities from previous years.

TABLE 9

STATE CREDITS FROM RUSSIA TO THE CIS STATES
IN THE SECOND HALF OF 1993
(*billions of rubles*)

Republics	Amount	Repayment Period
Armenia	20	1996–2000
Belarus	70	2001–2008
Kazakhstan	150	1995–1997
Kirghizstan	15	1994–1997
Moldova	50	1995–1998
Tajikistan	60	1996–2000
Ukraine	250	1994–1996
Uzbekistan	125	1996–2002
Total	740	

SOURCES: Russian Ministry of Finance and Center for Economic Reform.
NOTE: Credits announced on August 3, 1993. The interest rate on these credits was set to vary with LIBOR. For most credits, the rate was LIBOR + 1; for Tajikistan, it was LIBOR + 0.5, and for Uzbekistan, it was LIBOR + 1.5.

repay a technical credit due Russia, Russia refinanced the liability but converted it into dollars—to be reconverted to rubles at the time of payment at the exchange rate current then. In bilateral trade negotiations with Kazakhstan, Russia insisted that Kazakhstan's trade deficit with Russia be transformed into sovereign debt with conditions analogous to standard Western loans. The government of Kazakhstan was not prepared to do this, and an agreement on financing the trade deficit could not be reached. Prime Minister Sergei Tereschenko of Kazakhstan claimed that Russia's tough stance in the negotiations was intended to push Kazakhstan out of the ruble area (*Isvestiya*, June 22, 1993).

By introducing ceilings on overdrafts and the use of state credits, the exploitation of correspondent accounts for seigniorage gains was effectively ended. Payments clearing occurred through rationing, with the correspondent accounts of the various national banks at the CBR receiving accounting credits for exports to Russia. These credits could be used to settle bills for imports from Russia, but because imports from Russia invariably exceeded exports to Russia, payments "booked" at the commercial-bank level remained uncleared at the central-bank level. Cross-country arrears were one result.

The inconvertibility of accounting balances also led to efforts to keep transactions "off the books," because firms had no assurance that export receipts earned in accounting balances would be available to them for purchasing imports. In addition, large speculative opportunities arose from the discrepancies between the book values and market values of non-cash credits.

CBR insistence on regulation of members' central-bank activity. The payments-clearing mechanism provided the central banks of the ruble area (including the CBR) with a strategic incentive to monetize excessive fiscal deficits. Each central bank retained the ability to issue money through its control over non-cash credits and its use of ruble supplements. The CBR first attempted to curb this behavior through the informal coordination of central-bank credit policy.[22] This proved ineffective, however, and the CBR apparently concluded that restoration of convertibility in the ruble area could be ensured only by direct control over the currency and credit policies of ruble-area members. The CBR thus imposed ever-more-restrictive "rules" on the member central banks, rules that would have converted the banks into branches of the CBR had they been accepted. These restrictions provided additional impetus for countries to leave the ruble area.[23] Member countries were unwilling to agree to the Russian demands, although most of them continued to negotiate with Russia. The monetary reform of July 1993 (discussed below) forced the issue for the non-Russian members. Even though negotiations led, in September 1993, to a framework for a new type of ruble area, the restrictive conditions imposed by the CBR led most member states to introduce national currencies by the end of the year.

The CBR requirements for continued participation in the ruble area were laid out explicitly in communication with the NBB. In mid-June 1993, the chairman of the Russian Committee on Economic Relations with the Commonwealth of Independent States (CIS) set six conditions under which Belarus could receive ruble banknotes after July 1, 1993:

- The Russian ruble would be the only legal currency in Belarus;

---

[22] A ruble-zone agreement in early 1992 reportedly allowed each central bank to increase its issuance of credit by 300 percent over the year. This was predicated on a substantial decrease in real credit creation; at the time of the agreement, the official forecast of price inflation for the year was 600 percent.

[23] On June 16, 1993, Russian Deputy Prime Minister Alexander Shokhin urged the former Soviet republics either to hasten the introduction of new currencies or to adhere more strictly to Russian guidelines on monetary policies (*Kommersant*, June 17, 1993).

- The CBR would have the power to regulate NBB issuance of credits;
- Belarus' banking laws would be identical to those of Russia;
- Russian laws would be used to regulate commercial banks and hard-currency operations;
- Belarus would be part of Russia's interbank settlement system;
- Russian bodies would have control over the implementation of agreements.

If Belarus accepted these conditions, Russia would continue to provide rubles until October 1, 1993.

In effect, these conditions would have established the NBB as a regional branch of the CBR—reestablishing in large part the organizational structure of the Soviet Union. They would also have removed the opportunities for Belarus to set an independent seigniorage strategy, although seigniorage would presumably have accrued for those banknotes issued in Belarus. Other member states faced similar demands and negotiations.

The monetary reform of July 1993. On July 24, 1993, the CBR and the presidency of Russia announced that Soviet and Russian banknotes issued between 1961 and 1992 would be taken out of circulation at midnight the next day. Banknotes issued in 1993 and Soviet and Russian coins issued after 1961 were to remain in circulation. Members of the currency area were given no official warning of this move. Belarus, Kazakhstan, and Uzbekistan were generally supportive, declaring that they would remain in the ruble zone but would not phase out old ruble notes as rapidly as Russia. Armenia objected vehemently, reminding Russia that states in the ruble zone had agreed to give six months' advance warning of any national currency change. Azerbaijan planned to replace the old rubles with its new currency, the manat, and gave its national bank two days to work out the details. Georgia announced that it would accelerate its abandonment of the ruble by giving its citizens one week to exchange rubles for Georgian menati. Moldova also decided to hasten its introduction of the leu, withdrawing ruble notes with a value of 200 or more rubles as of July 26 but retaining lower-denomination ruble notes alongside Moldovan leu.

An August 4 *Kommersant* editorial suggested that the currency reform was an attempt to put an end to the ruble area: "Viktor Gerashchenko in two days solved a problem that the best minds of the Ministry of Finance had tackled for years." The reform eliminated from use in Russia the banknotes in circulation in the rest of the currency area and placed added pressure on the member central banks either to agree to more restrictive conditions for reconstitution of the ruble area or to be excluded from distributions of the new Russian rubles.[24]

Efforts to reform the ruble area. Attempts to reform the ruble area began in 1992. At the Bishkek meeting of central-bank presidents in May 1992, the Interbank Coordinating Council was created to discuss coordination of monetary policy and the creation of an interstate bank for clearing payments. The interstate bank was designed to separate the activities of payments clearing from those of cash emission. Its charter was approved by ten ruble-area members in January 1993 in Minsk, but ratification by the remaining members had not been completed by the end of 1993.[25]

At a meeting of heads of state of the CIS countries in Bishkek in October 1992, the governments adopted guidelines—designed with the assistance of the IMF—for a system of trade and payments within the CIS. The CBR opposed the system because it implied a loss of control over the destination of cash issue (*Kommersant*, May 18, 1992). Ruble supplements were not eliminated under the agreement, but their creation had to coincide with the monetary policies put forward by the Interbank Coordinating Council. The Bishkek meeting also called for the coordination of budgetary and taxation policy.

After further work (and the impetus offered by the Russian monetary reform of July 1993), representatives of the governments and central banks of Armenia, Belarus, Kazakhstan, Russia, Tajikistan, and Uzbekistan signed an agreement in September 1993 outlining measures for the creation of a new currency area. The document was complemented by bilateral accords between Russia and the other members on specific measures for unifying national monetary, fiscal, banking, and customs policies. The agreement permitted the circulation of national currencies in the signatory countries for a transitional period, but it required that the issue of these non-ruble currencies be strictly regulated. The majority of signatories did not follow through with this program but continued with plans to introduce independent currencies.

[24] Another rationale, related to the currency area, was given by CBR deputy chairman Alexander Khandruyev. He stated that the CBR had become concerned as Soviet-era rubles flowed into Russia from the non-Russian members for exchange for new Russian rubles and that it had, in early July 1993, announced a gradual elimination of Soviet-era rubles from circulation by the end of 1993. Mikhail Berger reported these details in the July 27 issue of *Isvestiya* but cited reasons in his commentary for distrusting this explanation of the CBR's motives.

[25] This issue of a clearing mechanism has not been settled quickly. In May 1995, the CIS summit had as one item of business a mechanism for settling interstate payments.

The evolving advice of the international financial organizations.
Throughout this period, ruble-area countries negotiated with the IMF
and the World Bank for membership in those organizations and for the
financial assistance associated with membership. The IMF took the
lead in advising the countries on financial matters. Citing the efficiency
advantages of a currency area, it initially urged members to remain
within the ruble area. It counseled Estonia not to introduce its own
currency as Estonia planned to do in June 1992 (Hansson and Sachs,
1992). Indeed, the IMF told "all [of the] countries that they would not
be entitled to IMF financing if they introduced their own currencies. It
[the IMF] was against every single currency reform, or at least stated
that they were premature, apart from the Kirghizstan currency reform
of 15 May 1993" (Åslund, 1994, p. 73). The advice of the IMF
changed, however, apparently in response to the success of Estonia's
currency program and to the continuing macroeconomic instability of
the remaining ruble-area countries. By mid-1993, the IMF was coun-
seling these countries to introduce independent currencies as quickly
as possible.

5   The Birth of Currencies

The birth of nations quickly triggered a competition for seigniorage
resources. The Baltic nations had planned from the beginning to leave
the currency area, had achieved fiscal balance, and had immediately
begun the introduction of national currencies. For the other countries,
the ruble area became a battleground for securing seigniorage resources.
Cash shortages and the inconvertibility of correspondent accounts were
inevitable results and the introduction of ruble supplements a logical
next step.

The pressure from the CBR to limit the independence of credit
policy in member countries placed added pressure on members to
reexamine their membership in the ruble area, and a number of
countries moved to introduce new currencies or to make existing ruble
supplements their only legal tender. By the time of the Russian currency
reform in July 1993, seven of the fifteen original members of the ruble
area had already broken away by introducing their own currencies.
Belarus and Georgia remained within the currency area but had ruble
supplements in circulation.

The recall of "old ruble" banknotes in July 1993 hastened the exit of
almost all the remaining members. Georgia broke with the ruble scarcely
a month after the recall. The others departed in quick succession,

40

beginning in November 1993. Turkmenistan led, followed shortly by Kazakhstan and Uzbekistan and then by Armenia and Moldova. Belarus also broke with the ruble area but almost simultaneously initialled an accord with Russia to reenter it. By the beginning of 1994, only Tajikistan among the original members remained with Russia in the currency area. Table 10 indicates when the ruble-area members introduced new currencies.

The timing of departure from the ruble area became a matter of strategic interest for the members, because the introduction of a new currency or other monetary reform in a neighboring country led to the flow of rubles across borders. In May 1993 in Kazakhstan, for example, the exchange rate of currency rubles to U.S. dollars diverged from that in Russia because rubles were flowing into Kazakhstan from Kirghizstan, where the government had introduced a new currency. On September 16, 1993, after the Russian currency reform, the Council Of Ministers of Kazakhstan introduced restrictions on the importation of "old rubles" into Kazakhstan from neighboring countries (*Kazakhstanskaya Pravda*, September 16, 1993). When Kazakhstan and Uzbekistan in turn introduced new currencies on November 15, 1993, reports the next week indicated a flood of "old rubles" into Tajikistan from these two neighbors.

The countries introducing independent currencies have differed greatly in subsequent satisfaction with their arrangements. Those states that introduced new currencies in conjunction with balanced fiscal budgets have reaped the benefits of low inflation and the relatively smooth integration of their new currencies into international financial markets. The majority of ruble-area states, however, introduced new currencies to provide seigniorage to cover fiscal deficits, and these countries have experienced high inflation, depreciation of their currencies relative to the ruble, and a lack of acceptance for their currencies on international markets.

The following sections examine four cases of currency introduction, in Estonia, Ukraine, Belarus, and Georgia. Estonia provides an example of currency introduction in conjunction with fiscal balance; Ukraine, Belarus, and Georgia all show large fiscal deficits met through seigniorage receipts. Ukraine was one of the first ruble-area countries to introduce a currency supplement and was also among the first to cease convertibility of the supplement with the ruble, thus creating a new currency de facto. Belarus introduced a currency supplement early as well but refused to leave the ruble area de jure, despite the large arbitrage opportunities that arose from trading rubles for supplements on official and private markets. It continued its pursuit of a renewed

41

TABLE 10

THE INTRODUCTION OF NEW CURRENCIES
IN THE FORMER SOVIET REPUBLICS

Republic	Supplement Introduced	New Currency Adopted	
		Date	Name
Armenia	—	November 1993	Dram
Azerbaijan	August 1992	June 1993	Manat
Belarus	May 1992	November 1993	Rubel
Estonia	—	June 1992	Kroon
Georgia[a]	April 1993	August 1993	Menati
Kazakhstan	—	November 1993	Tenge
Kirghizstan	—	May 1993	Som
Latvia[b]	May 1992	June 1993	Lats
Lithuania[c]	May 1992	June 1993	Litas
Moldova	July 1992	November 1993	Leu
Russia	—	—	—
Tajikistan	—	—	—
Turkmenistan	—	November 1993	Manat
Ukraine[a]	January 1992	November 1992	Karbovanets
Uzbekistan	November 1993	January 1994	Som

SOURCES: News reports.

[a] Georgia and Ukraine have announced that their present currencies, the menati and karbovanets, are temporary and that they are delaying the introduction of permanent currencies (the lari and hryvnia, respectively) until greater stability is achieved in the financial markets.

[b] The Latvian coupon (known as the Latvian ruble) became the sole currency of Latvia in August 1992 but was viewed as temporary. The lats, introduced in June 1993, is the permanent currency.

[c] The talonas was introduced by Lithuania as a coupon in May 1992. It became the sole currency in October 1992 but was replaced by the litas in June 1993.

currency union with Russia until the end of 1994. Georgia was late in introducing a currency supplement despite massive cash shortages. It subsequently made that supplement its sole legal tender, but commodity, service, and financial markets within Georgia have been nearly unanimous in their rejection of the supplement. Georgia remains, de facto, a member of the ruble area.

The success of a new currency can be judged by its acceptance and its stability in purchasing power. The four currencies considered below provide a spectrum of experience in this regard. The consumer-price inflation rates and exchange-rate movements indicate the relative variability in purchasing power. The degree of currency substitution illustrates nonacceptance of the currency as a medium of exchange or unit of account.[26]

Estonian Kroon: Introduction of a Viable Currency

Estonia was initially a member of the ruble area but suffered from cash shortages in early 1992 (see Table 7). For this reason, as well as for nationalist political reasons, Estonia introduced the kroon as its own currency on June 20 to 22, 1992. The kroon was introduced through conversion of 10 rubles to 1 kroon for bank balances, wages, prices, and other contracts, up to a limit of 1,500 rubles per resident. Rubles in excess of 1,500 traded at the ratio of 50 rubles per kroon. About 2.2 billion rubles in banknotes were redeemed and shipped back to Russia. The Russian and Estonian governments agreed to maintain intercountry trade financing and payments clearing in rubles.

The kroon was introduced with a fixed exchange rate of 8 to 1 vis-à-vis the German deutsche mark. The market exchange rate of rubles to deutsche marks at that time was about 75 to 1, so the fixed rate represented a slight depreciation. The initial official reserve holdings of the central bank (mostly monetary gold held in the West since 1939) more than equalled the money stock broadly defined (that is, M-2). The central bank's monetary policy was simply to ensure convertibility of the kroon for current-account transactions.

Introduction of the new currency was undertaken simultaneously with fiscal adjustment. The government restructured the tax system to raise additional revenues and reduced expenditures to achieve a balanced budget. The central-bank charter was then written to forbid the provision of credits to finance budget deficits; its activity was to be largely confined to foreign-exchange transactions at the fixed exchange rate. As Table 3 indicates, the fiscal accounts were in surplus in both 1992 and 1993.[27]

The new currency was a success in terms of both acceptance and stability. The kroon was convertible with the deutsche mark at a fixed exchange rate, whereas the ruble continued to depreciate against the

---

[26] In Ukraine, Georgia, and Belarus, I have, with in-country colleagues, collected information about the currency and commodity prices on a daily basis since early 1993. These data record daily observations of both formal and informal markets and form the basis of the discussion in this section. Further details about these data series are available from the author.

[27] Table 3 also shows that the fiscal surplus was larger in 1991. The surplus that year included transfers from the Soviet Union, however, so that fiscal retrenchment was necessary in 1992 even to attain the seemingly less favorable fiscal outcome reported here.

FIGURE 5

QUARTERLY INFLATION RATES IN FIVE FORMER REPUBLICS

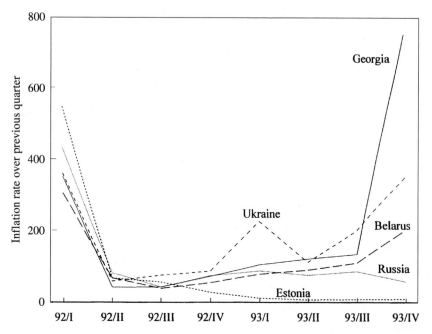

SOURCES: IMF, *International Financial Statistics*, and author's data-collection network.

deutsche mark. Currency shortages in Estonia disappeared, despite the strict rules on money creation imposed by the policy of convertibility. Inflation fell rapidly after a large burst in the first quarter of 1992 and remained substantially below that of the ruble area (Figure 5). The foreign-exchange reserves of the National Bank of Estonia expanded substantially.

Ukrainian Karbovanets: A New Currency de Facto

Ukraine declared its political independence in August 1991 but retained its membership in the ruble area. The Gosbank, however, unilaterally chose to make its last shipment of ruble banknotes to Ukraine at the end of September 1991. When Russia announced its plan to liberalize prices at the beginning of 1992, the Ukrainian authorities recognized the need for a ruble supplement. On January 10, 1992, the NBU issued the karbovanets as legal tender in state stores.[28] The karbovanets were

---

[28] This was not the first use of the karbovanets in Ukraine. It was first introduced as a single-use coupon in mid-1991 when controlled prices were raised throughout the Soviet

44

issued to Ukrainian wage earners, pensioners, and other residents in specific proportions; moreover, they could be purchased for hard currency at the exchange rate of 10 karbovanets to 1 U.S. dollar. The use of ruble notes was restricted to the payment of rents, transport fares, utilities and other services, and purchases in private markets.

"Karbovanets" is the Ukrainian word for "ruble" and was initially issued to exchange 1 for 1 with rubles. This was the case for non-cash transactions. The karbovanets bills, however, were not treated by the public as equal in value to cash rubles, and the NBU was unsuccessful at establishing free conversion between them; this conversion took place in informal markets.[29]

In the beginning, only 25 percent of wages and salaries were paid in karbovanets, with the balance paid in rubles. All food purchases, however, had to be made with karbovanets. Not surprisingly, therefore, a premium developed for karbovanets in informal markets, where the exchange rate was 4 rubles to 1 karbovanets. Over time, as the karbovanets bills were used to pay larger portions of wages and salaries, the karbovanets began to depreciate against the ruble in the informal markets. This depreciation was accelerated by the large fiscal deficits in Ukraine and the relatively restrictive monetary policy in Russia from January to April 1992, a combination that led to a trade imbalance and a flow of rubles out of Ukraine.[30] Although the Ukrainian cash karbovanets were trading at a discount to the ruble during the second quarter of 1992, the non-cash karbovanets and ruble credits continued to be exchanged at par. This encouraged Ukraine's trade deficit with Russia, because Ukrainians purchased karbovanets banknotes for rubles, deposited the banknotes in accounts, and used them to buy Russian goods and services.

Union. The rise in the prices of staples was not uniform across countries, and a vigorous cross-border arbitrage arose in these necessities. The karbovanets were distributed to Ukrainian citizens in sheets; to purchase staple goods, citizens presented both the requisite number of rubles and the requisite number of karbovanets clipped from the sheets. (This was the original rationale for referring to the karbovanets as a "coupon.") Because noncitizens did not receive the sheets, they could not purchase the goods for resale across the border. These karbovanets were not reused. The ruble supplement in Belarus began in a similar fashion, as noted below.

[29] This may have resulted from an unwillingness on the part of the NBU to give official recognition to either of two possible outcomes of official currency exchange, both of which it regarded as undesirable: a cash-ruble shortage at the par value or a depreciation of the karbovanets against the ruble if the exchange rate were allowed to float.

[30] During this period, the ruble appreciated against the U.S. dollar. The January exchange rate was 160 rubles per dollar; the April exchange rate was 80 rubles per dollar.

In May and July 1992, the CBR introduced the central payments-clearing mechanisms and correspondent-overdraft ceilings described in Section 4. On September 22, news sources reported that Russia had suspended ruble credits to Ukraine. This led to a rupture in the exchange parity and a depreciation of the karbovanets against the ruble (Figure 6).

On November 15, 1992, the karbovanets became Ukraine's sole legal tender, with all accounts denominated and all state transactions made in karbovanets. The government's demand for seigniorage continued unabated, however, and the NBU accommodated that demand by issuing directed credits and cash. In mid-1993, the NBU issued about 200 billion karbovanets in cash each month, compared with a total of 106 billion karbovanets in circulation in June 1992. Nevertheless, cash shortages began in April 1993 and became quite severe in May. On June 1, 1993, the NBU issued cash-conserving regulations to commercial banks. Companies were allowed to make cash transactions only up to a value of five times the minimum monthly wage bill; larger transactions had to be made through non-cash accounts. Unlimited cash withdrawals were allowed only for wages, salaries, and pensions. Cash withdrawals for other purposes were limited to fifteen times the minimum wage per month. Commercial banks were to encourage enterprises to pay wages through credits to accounts rather than in cash. Individuals, in turn, were allowed to use cash only for consumer goods valued at less than 138,000 karbovanets; otherwise, they were to pay through their bank accounts.

The karbovanets depreciated against the ruble from October 1992 to April 1993. In May and June, however, it appreciated against the ruble, in part because karbovanets were in short supply during that period. The NBU established an exchange rate for the karbovanets against the ruble and U.S. dollar for use in official transactions and held to that rate even though it was overvalued (Figure 6, top panel). The daily record of the exchange rate from April 14 through December 31, 1993 (Figure 6, bottom panel) shows the great discrepancy between market and NBU exchange rates. The depreciation of the karbovanets against the ruble gathered pace with the Russian currency reform of July 1993 and accelerated through August and September of that year. The gap between market and NBU rates grew larger.

Ukraine had an average quarterly inflation rate of roughly 100 percent from the second quarter of 1992 through the third quarter of 1993. As Figure 5 shows, this performance was the most inflationary of the four considered for that period. Indeed, it was the highest among the former Soviet republics. Hard currencies, U.S. dollars and deutsche

FIGURE 6
THE EXCHANGE RATE OF KARBOVANETS FOR RUBLES IN UKRAINE

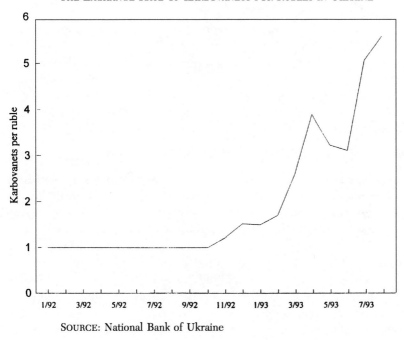

SOURCE: National Bank of Ukraine

SOURCE: Author's data-collection network.

marks, were in great demand as stores of value and for some commodity purchases, but the karbovanets retained its role as medium of exchange for the majority of transactions.

The Ukrainian government would like to introduce a permanent currency, which it has called the hryvnia. The NBU recognizes, however, that introducing the hryvnia during a period of inflation and exchange-rate depreciation would condemn it to the same hyperinflationary path as that followed by the karbovanets during 1992 and 1993. By the end of 1994, it seemed likely that the government could resolve its fiscal deficit and set the stage for introduction of the hryvnia.[31]

Belarus Ruble: A New Currency Reluctantly Introduced

The Belarus ruble, or zaichik, was initially introduced as a coupon in 1991 to protect domestic consumers from shortages resulting from the export of relatively lower priced staples to external markets.[32] It reappeared as a ruble supplement in 1992 in response to severe cash shortages.

The budget in Belarus was in deficit, although not so severely as in Georgia or Ukraine. Despite a strong tax-collection performance, the fiscal deficit grew each year, reaching 8.4 percent of GDP in 1993. It was financed mainly by the provision of non-cash credits through the formal financial system (see Table 4). This reliance on non-cash finance for seigniorage, combined with controlled nominal interest rates, caused severe shortages of banknotes in Belarus.

In May 1992, arrears in wage payments reached 4 billion rubles. The government reintroduced the zaichik on May 25, 1992, as a supplement to the Russian ruble, with a fixed exchange rate on cash purchases of 10 rubles per zaichik. From May to August 1992, there were no cash shortages. In October 1992, the government required that food, alcohol, and tobacco purchases be made in zaichik and that zaichik be the sole currency accepted at state shops in border areas.[33] By the end of 1992, zaichik represented about 80 percent of the currency in circulation in Belarus.

Because budget deficits continued to be financed by directed credits, cash shortages reappeared. In May and June of 1993, the shortage of

---

[31] On June 5, 1995, Reuters reported that President Leonid Kuchma had announced that the new currency will be introduced in the fall of 1995.

[32] "Zaichik" is the Belarus word for rabbit. Belarusians refer to the currency as the "zaichik" because the rabbit is on the one-ruble note. I use "zaichik" as a distinctive name for the currency and not in a derogatory way.

[33] This restriction remained in effect until May 1993, when it was abolished. There were no other restrictions on acceptance of rubles as opposed to zaichik.

cash in the currency markets was particularly acute (*Minsk Economic News*, August 1993). This shortage manifested itself in a large gap between the value of non-cash zaichik credits and cash. Non-cash zaichik exchanged at a rate of 1 to 5 with non-cash Russian rubles, whereas the banknotes of the two countries exchanged at a rate of 1 to 10. A speculative activity called "the mill" played on the wedge between Russian and Belarus credits. In July 1993, the exchange rate on the interbank market in Minsk was 18 Belarus non-cash zaichik for 100 non-cash Russian rubles. An individual with a non-cash ruble credit in a Moscow bank could trade this credit on the Interbank Currency Exchange in Minsk for 0.18 times its amount in non-cash zaichik. The Belarus banks converted non-cash zaichik to zaichik banknotes at par (when cash was available). The cash zaichik traded for cash rubles at 1 to 10. The rubles obtained in this way were then transported to Moscow and exchanged for 1.3 times as many non-cash Russian rubles (because cash traded at a premium to non-cash credits in that market as well). One cycle produced a 50 to 70 percent profit, even after payments for favorable treatment at the Belarus bank.

The supply of Russian rubles allocated to Belarus by the CBR was insufficient to service both transactions demand and this new arbitrage demand. Russian cash began to trade at a premium of 20 to 25 percent in informal markets. In formal banking operations, conversion of rubles for zaichik at par was rationed.

The Russian monetary reform in July 1993 hit hard in Belarus. Non-Russians were given one day to convert old Russian rubles to zaichik and were limited by a ceiling of 15,000 old rubles per person (in contrast to 100,000 rubles allowed each Russian in Russia). In Minsk, the zaichik depreciated strongly against the U.S. dollar, while the new Russian ruble appreciated in value. On November 18, 1993, the Belarus parliament ratified both the CIS economic union and an agreement to form a monetary union with Russia. Both agreements were passed by large majorities, although some opposed the monetary union because it required Belarus to surrender authority over its monetary and fiscal policy to Russia. During debates on the issue, Chairman of the Supreme Soviet Stanislau Shushkevich warned against ratification, whereas Prime Minister Vyacheslau Kebich urged deputies to ratify the union.

Quarterly inflation in Belarus increased steadily after the introduction of the zaichik in the second quarter of 1992 (see Figure 5). This led to a depreciation of the zaichik against the ruble in informal markets (see Figure 7 for the last half of 1993). The zaichik remained the medium of exchange for most commodity transactions, although shops appeared

49

FIGURE 7

THE EXCHANGE RATE OF ZAICHIK FOR RUBLES IN BELARUS

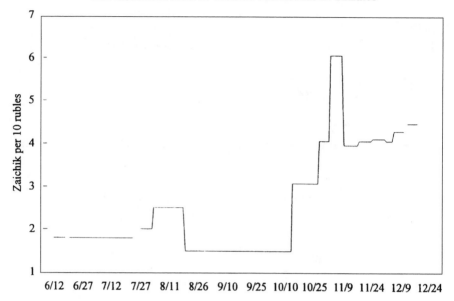

SOURCE: Author's data-collection network.

offering goods for sale in hard currencies. Hard currencies remained in demand as a store of value during this inflationary period.

Georgian Menati: A Currency de Jure But Not de Facto

Georgia remained a member of the ruble area following its independence in April 1991. It had large fiscal deficits, however, throughout the 1991-93 period (Table 3). The non-cash credits created to finance these deficits in the first half of 1992 greatly outstripped cash issue and the accumulation of saving deposits, leading to tremendous pressures for the provision of cash. There were substantial ruble cash shortages in Georgia from December 1992 to March 1993. These led to large arrears in the government's payments of pensions, income supplements, and public-sector wages. Private enterprises also found it difficult to obtain cash rubles. The NBG issued directives to banks on a number of occasions to conserve the use of rubles by limiting the release of cash to depositors (see Section 4).

Georgia introduced its ruble supplement, the menati, on April 5, 1993. It was used to pay wages, salaries, and pensions, including sums unpaid since December 1992 because of the insufficient supply of rubles. The menati was priced at par with the ruble and could be used for all purchases except for those goods originally purchased with rubles (for example, petrol and other imports from Russia).

The menati was originally issued in denominations of 10, 50, 1,000, and 5,000. The absence of small bills led to initial confusion, because consumers purchasing goods with menati had to accept change in rubles. Currency trading in informal markets was initially extremely light, with the menati trading at a premium to the ruble in the few observed cases. Thereafter, for the first two weeks after introduction, the menati and ruble traded at par. The issuance of menati, however, led to initial food-price increases of approximately 20 percent as pent-up demand was released from forced saving.

Even in the first weeks, however, the menati was not universally accepted, and many shopkeepers would not accept it in payment. The stability and acceptance of the menati weakened further during the following months. Although the government traded in official foreign-exchange markets at menati-ruble parity and decreed that all privatiza-tion purchases must be made in menati, many merchants insisted upon cash rubles or accepted menati only at a steep discount.[34] State shops continued to sell rationed goods (bread, butter, macaroni, sugar) for menati at par with rubles, but these goods were in short supply.

The government responded (in a speech by the deputy prime minis-ter to parliament on June 10, 1993) by insisting that the menati and ruble would continue to trade at par and that exchange outside NBG exchange offices would be illegal. Nevertheless, informal transactions continued, and the menati depreciated rapidly against the ruble. There was also a progressive shift away from use of the menati in transac-tions.[35] The system of state shops disintegrated, with many either

[34] The Committee for Social and Economic Information in Georgia conducted a study on April 21, 1993 (that is, twelve days after issuance) to examine the effectiveness of the menati as a medium of exchange. Twenty-nine commodities and services were chosen for study, and representatives of the committee visited sellers of these in three sectors: state and cooperative outlets, commercial shops, and the bazaar. State shops honored the menati at par with the ruble, but eight goods were "out of stock"; forty-two percent of commercial shops would not accept menati; and 66 percent of the sellers interviewed in the bazaar would not accept menati.

[35] A government investigation in Tbilisi on July 21 found that 60 percent of a sample of 52 commodities and services were not available for purchase in menati at state and cooperative shops, and 55 percent of commodities and services were not available for menati in private shops, despite a roughly 50 percent markup in menati prices over ruble prices. Only in the bazaar were foodstuffs available for menati, but there, the accepted exchange rate was 5 menati to the ruble.

closing or becoming privatized. For example, the central department store in Tbilisi was partitioned, and a number of its departments became commercial shops. Other commercial shops also opened, including a growing number of hard-currency boutiques that refused to accept menati. These latter priced Western goods in U.S. dollars and CIS goods in rubles.

The final blow to the fiction that the menati and ruble were perfect substitutes came with the Russian monetary reform in July 1993. The Georgian government decided then to remove the ruble as legal tender in Georgia and decreed that, as of August 2, the ruble would no longer be accepted as domestic currency. Exchange offices were set up throughout the country to handle the exchange of foreign currencies (including the ruble) for menati. Informal trading of foreign currencies became illegal.

This monetary reform was not linked to a revision of the budget, however, and the Georgian government remained in deep fiscal deficit. Ongoing disputes between the government in Tbilisi and the leaders of provinces seeking autonomy in Ossetia and Abkhazia led to strife requiring military intervention; in Abkhazia, the conflict became a civil war requiring international peacekeeping intervention. Refugees from these regions poured into the areas under government control, leading to increased expenses for support services. There were also large costs associated with the cleanup from the coup of late 1991 that removed President Gamsakhurdia. For all of these reasons, as well as a collapse of the tax-collection system (see Table 3), the government's demand for seigniorage became insatiable.

By the end of September, the menati had become a least-preferred currency for most transactions. State shops for commodities had disappeared, and commercial shops had obtained licenses to transact in any currency, despite the menati's position as sole legal tender. The only commodities sold for menati were bread and the rations of sugar and butter, and these were also available in informal markets for other currencies.

The depreciation of the menati had an extreme effect on the Georgian population, whose salaries represent strikingly low purchasing power. The newspaper *Droni* reported on November 18, 1993, that the prime minister's entire monthly salary was convertible to $2.27 at the then-current exchange rate—yet prices for commodities had not decreased in terms of foreign currencies. Figure 8 shows the quantity of beef that could be purchased with $1 in the bazaar during 1993. Although it is quite variable, it shows no trend when defined in dollar terms. In

FIGURE 8

THE NOMINAL AND REAL EXCHANGE RATES OF MENATI FOR RUBLES IN GEORGIA

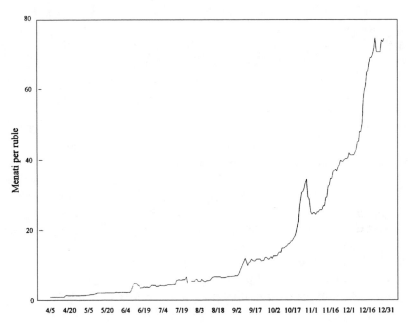

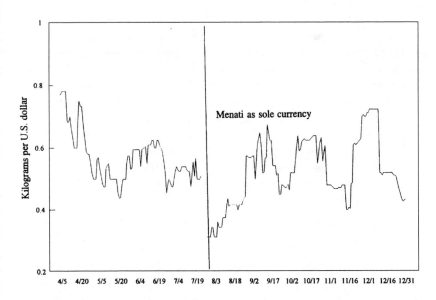

Menati as sole currency

SOURCE: Author's data-collection network.

menati, however, the prime minister's monthly salary in menati could have purchased only slightly more than 1 kilogram of beef at the end of December, and even then, not directly: the merchants in the bazaar would not accept menati.

Although inflation was substantial throughout the postindependence period (see Figure 5), it steadily increased through late 1992 and 1993, until it exploded in the fourth quarter of 1993. Menati were in little demand, either for exchange or for saving. The ruble was the de facto currency of Georgia.

One of the signals of inconvertibility that prompted the introduction of the menati in Georgia was the imbalance in valuation between non-cash and cash holdings. Figure 9 illustrates this imbalance for the April-December period in 1993 by calculating the premium for cash over non-cash in the foreign-exchange market. In early April, cash in Georgia was worth six to eight times as much as non-cash credits with equivalent face value. The introduction of the menati led to a reduction in this imbalance, but in April, the premium still remained above 200 percent. By June, cash evidenced a 100 percent premium, and this wedge remained after the elimination of the ruble as legal tender. It was only with the massive cash emissions from October through December that the premium was driven toward zero, although even in December, the premium on cash was 33 percent.

Banknotes for the new Georgian currency, the lari, were ordered in January 1993, but officials of the NBG had indicated that the budget must be improved and recession ended before the new currency was introduced. Because these preconditions had not been met in 1993, the currency was kept on the shelf. In late 1993, Georgia joined the CIS, a move interpreted by observers as (among other things) a step toward monetary reintegration with Russia. In January 1994, parliament chairman Eduard Shevardnadze admitted on Georgian television that circulating the menati in 1993 in tandem with the ruble had been "a costly error," but he insisted that Georgia needed several months to consider whether to rejoin the ruble zone. He did not at that time discuss the lari.

7 Conclusions

The ruble area disintegrated rapidly after the dissolution of the Soviet Union. For the Baltic states, the introduction of new currencies was an anticipated event, prepared for by appropriate fiscal adjustment. For the non-Baltic states, the introduction of new currencies was more

54

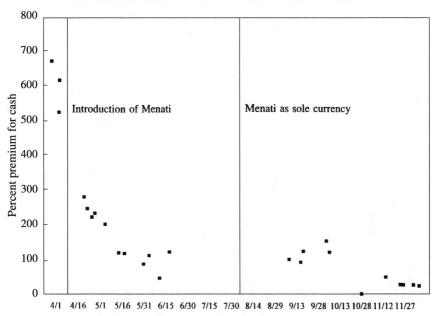

FIGURE 9

THE PREMIUM FOR CASH OVER NON-CASH CREDITS IN GEORGIA

SOURCE: Author's data-collection network.

haphazard and was driven by the need for additional seigniorage to meet fiscal imbalances. The emission and distribution of ruble banknotes by the CBR were insufficient to meet their demand.

Many of the ruble-area members dealt with cash shortages by introducing ruble supplements. These supplements were intended to trade at par with the ruble, but they were never convertible at par across countries and quickly lost parity in unofficial transactions within each country. Only in the Baltic states did the supplements trade at a premium vis-à-vis the ruble; in the non-Baltic countries, the supplements traded at a discount.

Two channels of additional public finance emerged in this environment of fiscal imbalance. First, each government began using directed credits to finance its purchases. Although these credits created non-cash purchasing power for the governments, they quickly lost convertibility at par across countries and with cash within each country. Rationing was imposed through limits on overdrafts of correspondent accounts at the CBR and on the cash that domestic banks could provide in exchange for non-cash deposits. Second, the government of Russia

55

provided technical credits, and later state credits, to clear persistent correspondent overdrafts of the non-Russian members. With the technical credits, the Russian government provided these members with needed seigniorage; with the state credits, it provided financing for fiscal deficits, in part through high-cost international borrowing.

By mid-1993, the Russian government and the CBR were rethinking their attitude toward the currency area. After initially assisting those countries wishing to stay within the currency area, the CBR began in mid-1993 to demand more influence over the credit-creating activities of national banks in member countries. At the same time, the CBR converted Russian credits to clear correspondent accounts from ruble-denominated to U.S. dollar-denominated credits and began to charge interest rates based on the London Interbank Offer Rate (LIBOR). The CBR also discouraged continued participation in the ruble area by its July 1993 monetary reform. This reform not only created difficulties in the conversion of ruble banknotes, it also warned the member central banks that the CBR was ready and able to take noncollegial decisions regarding currency circulation. International financial institutions underwent a similar change in their attitudes. Their representatives switched from encouraging participation in the currency area to encouraging the delinking of currencies.

By the end of 1993, the need for seigniorage in the non-Baltic states had run headlong into the unwillingness of the CBR to provide sufficient banknotes or to honor directed credits created by member national banks. In this situation, fiscal imbalance pushed members inexorably toward the introduction of new currencies or the declaration that existing supplements would be sole legal tender. The results were predictable but disheartening. Inflation in these countries exceeded that in Russia; the new currencies depreciated against the ruble; and the national central banks had difficulty ensuring the convertibility of the new currencies into "hard" currencies or rubles.

This essay considers only the period up to the end of 1993. Although by that time, the explosion of the ruble area was largely complete, the year 1994 brought some interesting postscripts to the analysis, especially for the four case studies considered. The CBR in Russia, led by Geraschenko until the ruble crisis of October 1994, was remarkably successful in reining in inflationary pressure in the first half of the year. Much of its success could be credited to the newfound resolve of the Russian government to move toward fiscal balance in its spending program. Ukraine and Belarus held presidential elections, and in each case, the successful candidate was the one campaigning for closer union, including monetary union, with Russia. In both countries, there was some effort toward resolution of the fiscal imbalance through expenditure reduction and tax reform. In Ukraine, this began in early 1994 and yielded a drastic reduction in inflation; in Belarus, it began only under the new president, Alexander Lukashenka. The notion of reentry to the ruble area was shelved, because both governments (in addition to Russia's) recognized the need for fiscal harmonization before any new monetary integration could be successful. In Georgia, the political situation was stabilized, but the menati remained a currency little accepted in its own country. Estonia continued to consolidate its gains from the creation of a stable currency.

The explosion of the ruble area has a historical precedent. As Garber and Spencer (1994) and Åslund (1994) note, the experience of the Austro-Hungarian Empire was quite similar. Fiscal deficits in Austria were monetized in the common currency, causing inflation throughout the former empire. Hungary, Czechoslovakia, and the other constituent nations introduced currency reforms to insulate their economies from that inflation and were by consequence able to follow policies of varying reliance on seigniorage in financing fiscal deficits.

The ruble area, in turn, provides guidance regarding the requirements for a successful European monetary union. The parallels are not complete. The governments of Western Europe have better access than the former Soviet republics have to international credit markets and are therefore less reliant on seigniorage for finance. In addition, the structural adjustments to be made in Western Europe are not as profound as those necessary in the former Soviet Union, although the integration of Germany is an analogous process. Nevertheless, the lesson of the ruble area's demise is significant for Western Europe. Monetary union requires fiscal coordination and fiscal restraint. The history of the ruble area shows in stark form the perils of attempting monetary integration with independent central banks and uncoordinated fiscal policies.

References

Åslund, Anders, "Key Dilemmas in the Russian Economic Reform," Stockholm, Stockholm School of Economics, 1993, processed.
——, panelist, in Bretton Woods Commission, Bretton Woods: Looking to the Future, Washington, D.C., Bretton Woods Commission, 1994. pp. 72-74.
Bayoumi, Tamim, "A Formal Model of Optimum Currency Areas," CEPR Discussion Paper No. 968, London, Centre for Economic Policy Research, June 1994.

Blanchard, Olivier, and Stanley Fischer, *Lectures on Macroeconomics*, Cambridge, Mass., MIT Press, 1989.

Buiter, Willem, and Jonathan Eaton, "International Balance of Payments Financing and Adjustment," in George von Furstenburg, ed., *International Money and Credit: The Policy Roles*, Washington, D.C., International Monetary Fund, 1983, pp. 129-148.

Canzoneri, Matthew, and Dale Henderson, *Monetary Policy in Interdependent Economies: A Game-Theoretic Approach*, Cambridge, Mass., MIT Press, 1991.

Canzoneri, Matthew, and Carol Rogers, "Is the European Union an Optimal Currency Area? Optional Taxation versus Cost of Multiple Currencies," *American Economic Review*, 80 (June 1990), pp. 419-433.

Casella, Alessandra, "Participation in a Currency Union," *American Economic Review*, 82 (September 1992), pp. 847-863.

Central Bank of Russia (CBR), *Bulletin of Banking Statistics*, Moscow, Central Bank of Russia, various issues.

Conway, Patrick, *Economic Shocks and Structural Adjustments: Turkey after 1973*, Amsterdam and New York, North-Holland, 1987.

———, "An Atheoretic Evaluation of Success in Structural Adjustment," *Economic Development and Cultural Change*, 42 (January 1994a), pp. 267-292.

———, "Rubles, Rubles Everywhere . . . Currency Shortages and Financial Disintermediation in the former Soviet Union," Chapel Hill, N.C., University of North Carolina, 1994b, processed.

———, "Sustained Inflation in Response to Price Liberalization," World Bank Policy Research Working Paper No. 1368, Washington, D.C., World Bank, 1994c.

Council of Economic Advisors, *Economic Report of the President*, Washington, D.C., Government Printing Office, January 1993.

Corden, W. Max, *Monetary Integration*, Princeton Essays in International Finance No. 93, Princeton, N.J., Princeton University, International Finance Section, April 1972.

Cukierman, Alex, *Central Bank Strategy, Credibility and Independence*, Cambridge, Mass., MIT Press, 1992.

De Grauwe, Paul, *The Economics of Monetary Integration*, Oxford, Oxford University Press, 1992.

Dornbusch, Rudiger, "Lessons from Experiences with High Inflation," *World Bank Economic Review*, 6 (January 1992), pp. 13-31.

Eichengreen, Barry, "European Monetary Unification," *Journal of Economic Literature*, 31 (September 1993), pp. 1321-1357.

Friedman, James, *Game Theory with Applications to Economics*, 2d edition, New York, Oxford University Press, 1990.

Garber, Peter, and Michael Spencer, *The Dissolution of the Austro-Hungarian Empire: Lessons for Currency Reform*, Princeton Essays in International Finance No. 191, Princeton, N.J., Princeton University, International Finance Section, February 1994.

Goldstein, Morris, Peter Isard, Paul Masson, and Mark Taylor: *Policy Issues in the Evolving International Monetary System*, Occasional Paper No. 96, Washington, D.C., International Monetary Fund, June 1992..

Goskomstat-USSR, *Narodnoe Khozaistvo SSSR v 1990 g*, Moscow, Goskomstat, 1991.

Gregory, Paul, and Robert Stuart, *Soviet Economic Structure and Performance*, 4th edition, New York, Harper & Row, 1990.

Hansson, Ardo, "Transforming an Economy while Building a Nation: The Case of Estonia," Stockholm, Stockholm Institute of East European Economics, 1992, processed.

Hansson, Ardo, and Jeffrey Sachs: "Crowning the Estonian Kroon," *Transition*, 3 (October 1992), pp. 1-2.

Hogan, William, "Economic Reforms in the Sovereign States of the Former Soviet Union," *Brookings Papers on Economic Activity*, No. 2 (1991), pp. 303-319.

Ickes, Barry, and Randi Ryterman, "Financial Underdevelopment and Macroeconomic Stabilization in Russia," in Gerald Caprio, David Folkerts-Landau, and Timothy Lane, eds., *Building Sound Finance in Emerging Market Economies*, Washington, D.C., International Monetary Fund, 1994.

International Monetary Fund, *International Financial Statistics*, Washington, D.C., International Monetary Fund, various issues.

Ishiyama, Yoshihide, "The Theory of Optimum Currency Areas: A Survey," *International Monetary Fund Staff Papers*, 22 (July 1975), pp. 344-383.

Kazakhstan, Cabinet of Ministers, Resolution No. 783, "On Strengthening the Control of Cash Money Coming from Enterprises and Organizations of All Forms of Property to the Cashiers' Offices of Banks," Alma-Ata, Kazakhstan, June 8, 1993.

Kenen, Peter, "Transitional Arrangements for Trade and Payments among the CMEA Countries," International Monetary Fund Staff Papers, 38 (June 1991), pp. 235-267; reprinted as Reprints in International Finance No. 27, Princeton, N.J., Princeton University, International Finance Section, July 1991.

Lipton, David, and Jeffrey Sachs, "Prospects for Russia's Economic Reform," *Brookings Papers on Economic Activity*, 2 (1992), pp. 213-265.

McKinnon, Ronald, *The Order of Economic Liberalization: Financial Control in the Transition to a Market Economy*, Baltimore, The Johns Hopkins University Press, 1991.

Rutland, Peter, and Timur Isataev, "Kazakhstan," in Michael Wyzan, ed., *First Steps toward Economic Independence: The New States of the Post-Communist World*, Westport, Conn., Greenwood, 1995.

Sala-i-Martin, Xavier, and Jeffrey Sachs: "Fiscal Federalism and Optimum Currency Areas: Evidence for Europe from the United States," in Matthew Canzoneri, Vittorio Grilli, and Paul Masson, eds., *Establishing a Central Bank: Issues in Europe and Lessons from the US*, Cambridge and New York, Cambridge University Press, 1992, pp. 195-219.

Tavlas, George, "The Theory of Optimum Currency Areas Revisited," *Finance and Development*, 30 (June 1993), pp. 32-35.

von Hagen, Jürgen, "Fiscal Arrangements in a Monetary Union—Evidence from the US," in Donald Fair and Christian de Boissieu, eds., *Fiscal Policy, Taxation and the Financial System in an Increasingly Integrated Europe*, Dordrecht and Boston, Kluwer, 1992, pp. 337-359

PUBLICATIONS OF THE
INTERNATIONAL FINANCE SECTION

Notice to Contributors

The International Finance Section publishes papers in four series: ESSAYS IN INTERNATIONAL FINANCE, PRINCETON STUDIES IN INTERNATIONAL FINANCE, and SPECIAL PAPERS IN INTERNATIONAL ECONOMICS contain new work not published elsewhere. REPRINTS IN INTERNATIONAL FINANCE reproduce journal articles previously published by Princeton faculty members associated with the Section. The Section welcomes the submission of manuscripts for publication under the following guidelines:

ESSAYS are meant to disseminate new views about international financial matters and should be accessible to well-informed nonspecialists as well as to professional economists. Technical terms, tables, and charts should be used sparingly; mathematics should be avoided.

STUDIES are devoted to new research on international finance, with preference given to empirical work. They should be comparable in originality and technical proficiency to papers published in leading economic journals. They should be of medium length, longer than a journal article but shorter than a book.

SPECIAL PAPERS are surveys of research on particular topics and should be suitable for use in undergraduate courses. They may be concerned with international trade as well as international finance. They should also be of medium length.

Manuscripts should be submitted in triplicate, typed single sided and double spaced throughout on 8½ by 11 white bond paper. Publication can be expedited if manuscripts are computer keyboarded in WordPerfect 5.1 or a compatible program. Additional instructions and a style guide are available from the Section.

How to Obtain Publications

The Section's publications are distributed free of charge to college, university, and public libraries and to nongovernmental, nonprofit research institutions. Eligible institutions may ask to be placed on the Section's permanent mailing list.

Individuals and institutions not qualifying for free distribution may receive all publications for the calendar year for a subscription fee of $40.00. Late subscribers will receive all back issues for the year during which they subscribe. Subscribers should notify the Section promptly of any change in address, giving the old address as well as the new.

Publications may be ordered individually, with payment made in advance. ESSAYS and REPRINTS cost $8.00 each; STUDIES and SPECIAL PAPERS cost $11.00. An additional $1.50 should be sent for postage and handling within the United States, Canada, and Mexico; $1.75 should be added for surface delivery outside the region.

All payments must be made in U.S. dollars. Subscription fees and charges for single issues will be waived for organizations and individuals in countries where foreign-exchange regulations prohibit dollar payments.

Please address all correspondence, submissions, and orders to:

International Finance Section
Department of Economics, Fisher Hall
Princeton University
Princeton, New Jersey 08544-1021

List of Recent Publications

A complete list of publications may be obtained from the International Finance Section.

ESSAYS IN INTERNATIONAL FINANCE

162. Stephen E. Haynes, Michael M. Hutchison, and Raymond F. Mikesell, *Japanese Financial Policies and the U.S. Trade Deficit.* (April 1986)
163. Arminio Fraga, *German Reparations and Brazilian Debt: A Comparative Study.* (July 1986)
164. Jack M. Guttentag and Richard J. Herring, *Disaster Myopia in International Banking.* (September 1986)
165. Rudiger Dornbusch, *Inflation, Exchange Rates, and Stabilization.* (October 1986)
166. John Spraos, *IMF Conditionality: Ineffectual, Inefficient, Mistargeted.* (December 1986)
167. Rainer Stefano Masera, *An Increasing Role for the ECU: A Character in Search of a Script.* (June 1987)
168. Paul Mosley, *Conditionality as Bargaining Process: Structural-Adjustment Lending, 1980-86.* (October 1987)
169. Paul A. Volcker, Ralph C. Bryant, Leonhard Gleske, Gottfried Haberler, Alexandre Lamfalussy, Shijuro Ogata, Jesús Silva-Herzog, Ross M. Starr, James Tobin, and Robert Triffin, *International Monetary Cooperation: Essays in Honor of Henry C. Wallich.* (December 1987)
170. Shafiqul Islam, *The Dollar and the Policy-Performance-Confidence Mix.* (July 1988)
171. James M. Boughton, *The Monetary Approach to Exchange Rates: What Now Remains?* (October 1988)
172. Jack M. Guttentag and Richard M. Herring, *Accounting for Losses On Sovereign Debt: Implications for New Lending.* (May 1989)
173. Benjamin J. Cohen, *Developing-Country Debt: A Middle Way.* (May 1989)
174. Jeffrey D. Sachs, *New Approaches to the Latin American Debt Crisis.* (July 1989)
175. C. David Finch, *The IMF: The Record and the Prospect.* (September 1989)
176. Graham Bird, *Loan-Loss Provisions and Third-World Debt.* (November 1989)
177. Ronald Findlay, *The "Triangular Trade" and the Atlantic Economy of the Eighteenth Century: A Simple General-Equilibrium Model.* (March 1990)
178. Alberto Giovannini, *The Transition to European Monetary Union.* (November 1990)
179. Michael L. Mussa, *Exchange Rates in Theory and in Reality.* (December 1990)
180. Warren L. Coats, Jr., Reinhard W. Furstenberg, and Peter Isard, *The SDR System and the Issue of Resource Transfers.* (December 1990)
181. George S. Tavlas, *On the International Use of Currencies: The Case of the Deutsche Mark.* (March 1991)
182. Tommaso Padoa-Schioppa, ed., with Michael Emerson, Kumiharu Shigehara, and Richard Portes, *Europe After 1992: Three Essays.* (May 1991)

183. Michael Bruno, *High Inflation and the Nominal Anchors of an Open Economy*. (June 1991)

184. Jacques J. Polak, *The Changing Nature of IMF Conditionality*. (September 1991)

185. Ethan B. Kapstein, *Supervising International Banks: Origins and Implications of the Basle Accord*. (December 1991)

186. Alessandro Giustiniani, Francesco Papadia, and Daniela Porciani, *Growth and Catch-Up in Central and Eastern Europe: Macroeconomic Effects on Western Countries*. (April 1992)

187. Michele Fratianni, Jürgen von Hagen, and Christopher Waller, *The Maastricht Way to EMU*. (June 1992)

188. Pierre-Richard Agénor, *Parallel Currency Markets in Developing Countries: Theory, Evidence, and Policy Implications*. (November 1992)

189. Beatriz Armendariz de Aghion and John Williamson, *The G-7's Joint-and-Several Blunder*. (April 1993)

190. Paul Krugman, *What Do We Need to Know About the International Monetary System?* (July 1993)

191. Peter M. Garber and Michael G. Spencer, *The Dissolution of the Austro-Hungarian Empire: Lessons for Currency Reform*. (February 1994)

192. Raymond F. Mikesell, *The Bretton Woods Debates: A Memoir*. (March 1994)

193. Graham Bird, *Economic Assistance to Low-Income Countries: Should the Link be Resurrected?* (July 1994)

194. Lorenzo Bini-Smaghi, Tommaso Padoa-Schioppa, and Francesco Papadia, *The Transition to EMU in the Maastricht Treaty*. (November 1994)

195. Ariel Buira, *Reflections on the International Monetary System*. (January 1995)

196. Shinji Takagi, *From Recipient to Donor: Japan's Official Aid Flows, 1945 to 1990 and Beyond*. (March 1995)

197. Patrick Conway, *Currency Proliferation: The Monetary Legacy of the Soviet Union*. (June 1995)

PRINCETON STUDIES IN INTERNATIONAL FINANCE

57. Stephen S. Golub, *The Current-Account Balance and the Dollar: 1977-78 and 1983-84*. (October 1986)

58. John T. Cuddington, *Capital Flight: Estimates, Issues, and Explanations*. (December 1986)

59. Vincent P. Crawford, *International Lending, Long-Term Credit Relationships, and Dynamic Contract Theory*. (March 1987)

60. Thorvaldur Gylfason, *Credit Policy and Economic Activity in Developing Countries with IMF Stabilization Programs*. (August 1987)

61. Stephen A. Schuker, *American "Reparations" to Germany, 1919-33: Implications for the Third-World Debt Crisis*. (July 1988)

62. Steven B. Kamin, *Devaluation, External Balance, and Macroeconomic Performance: A Look at the Numbers*. (August 1988)

63. Jacob A. Frenkel and Assaf Razin, *Spending, Taxes, and Deficits: International-Intertemporal Approach*. (December 1988)

64. Jeffrey A. Frankel, *Obstacles to International Macroeconomic Policy Coordination*. (December 1988)

65. Peter Hooper and Catherine L. Mann, *The Emergence and Persistence of the U.S. External Imbalance, 1980-87.* (October 1989)
66. Helmut Reisen, *Public Debt, External Competitiveness, and Fiscal Discipline in Developing Countries.* (November 1989)
67. Victor Argy, Warwick McKibbin, and Eric Siegloff, *Exchange-Rate Regimes for a Small Economy in a Multi-Country World.* (December 1989)
68. Mark Gersovitz and Christina H. Paxson, *The Economies of Africa and the Prices of Their Exports.* (October 1990)
69. Felipe Larraín and Andrés Velasco, *Can Swaps Solve the Debt Crisis? Lessons from the Chilean Experience.* (November 1990)
70. Kaushik Basu, *The International Debt Problem, Credit Rationing and Loan Pushing: Theory and Experience.* (October 1991)
71. Daniel Gros and Alfred Steinherr, *Economic Reform in the Soviet Union: Pas de Deux between Disintegration and Macroeconomic Destabilization.* (November 1991)
72. George M. von Furstenberg and Joseph P. Daniels, *Economic Summit Declarations, 1975-1989: Examining the Written Record of International Cooperation.* (February 1992)
73. Ishac Diwan and Dani Rodrik, *External Debt, Adjustment, and Burden Sharing: A Unified Framework.* (November 1992)
74. Barry Eichengreen, *Should the Maastricht Treaty Be Saved?* (December 1992)
75. Adam Klug, *The German Buybacks, 1932-1939: A Cure for Overhang?* (November 1993)
76. Tamim Bayoumi and Barry Eichengreen, *One Money or Many? Analyzing the Prospects for Monetary Unification in Various Parts of the World.* (September 1994)
77. Edward E. Leamer, *The Heckscher-Ohlin Model in Theory and Practice.* (February 1995)
78. Thorvaldur Gylfason, *The Macroeconomics of European Agriculture.* (May 1995)

SPECIAL PAPERS IN INTERNATIONAL ECONOMICS

16. Elhanan Helpman, *Monopolistic Competition in Trade Theory.* (June 1990)
17. Richard Pomfret, *International Trade Policy with Imperfect Competition.* (August 1992)
18. Hali J. Edison, *The Effectiveness of Central-Bank Intervention: A Survey of the Literature After 1982.* (July 1993)

REPRINTS IN INTERNATIONAL FINANCE

26. Peter B. Kenen, *The Use of IMF Credit*; reprinted from *Pulling Together: The International Monetary Fund in a Multipolar World,* 1989. (December 1989)
27. Peter B. Kenen, *Transitional Arrangements for Trade and Payments Among the CMEA Countries*; reprinted from *International Monetary Fund Staff Papers* 38 (2), 1991. (July 1991)
28. Peter B. Kenen, *Ways to Reform Exchange-Rate Arrangements*; reprinted from *Bretton Woods: Looking to the Future,* 1994. (November 1994)